The Message Maker

Kim,

It was a blessing speaking with you today at Emmaus House... I could sense our hearts as mothers connect!!! My prayer is that you feel the arms of Jesus wrapping around you, as you read the words of The Message Maker...

In Him,

Leta Rae Pereira

2/25/23

The Message Maker

Leta Rae Pereira

CROSSBOOKS
PUBLISHING

CrossBooks™
A Division of LifeWay
1663 Liberty Drive
Bloomington, IN 47403
www.crossbooks.com
Phone: 1-866-879-0502

First published by CrossBooks 12/12/2012

ISBN: 978-1-4627-2344-7 (sc)
ISBN: 978-1-4627-2345-4 (e)
ISBN: 978-1-4627-2346-1 (hc)

Library of Congress Control Number: 2012922083

Spirit-Filled Life®Mission Statement
The mission of *Spirit-Filled* Life Bibles and reference
products is to serve the body of Christ with a
broad range of trustworthy products marked by biblical
soundness, balanced scholarship and a
sense of honor toward the modern-day working of the
Holy Spirit. These resources are designed to
provide biblical equipping for practical living in God's kingdom and around the world.

Printed in the United States of America

This book is printed on acid-free paper.

Foreword

The Message Maker is not just a book to be read but an incredible journey that reaches into the deep places of your heart.

Leta's inspirational writings will stir you, challenge you, and remind you that we have a Father that longs to bring comfort and hope to His children.

As I read through the pages, I realized that each poem represented experiences we can all relate to and identify with; it felt like God was speaking to me in a very personal way.

The Message Maker is like sitting at a banquet table that will feed the longing of your soul. May you enjoy this book that is full of God's grace and truth as you hear the whisper of what the pages have to say.

Co-Pastor Dori Bannister
Hillside Christian Fellowship
Hollister, California

Introduction

In late December of 2008, there were "rumblings" within my spirit. At the time, I perceived them to be nudges from the Lord to maybe, someday, write a book, maybe about my life. Maybe someday. I thought it might be a possibility, as I kept hearing the words "Come, follow Me" off and on over the course of a few days. And I thought, "Yes, Lord, one day I will write my life's story because it's all about You, and I would love to share what You have done!" I had no idea that within a few short days, "someday" would become "now" and that the book I was possibly envisioning *would* unfold, not as my life's story but as poem after poem of "messages," messages sent straight from the gate of heaven. This is how it all began:

At about two in the morning on January 3, 2009, I was awakened from a sound sleep. (I know the Lord has a sense of humor because I have been blessed to be able to "sleep like a rock." I believe this was His way of telling me, "You know this is Me because nothing else would wake you up!") Immediately upon waking, I "saw" words written within my spirit: "Come, follow Me, My child. I will be with you from the start." I knew without a doubt that I was to begin writing. I remember looking for anything to write on and found a small piece of paper. Within a few minutes, I was searching for more paper, as I had nine verses! As I was writing them down, I suddenly realized that they were "memorized" within my spirit. This was all during the night of January 3. No more verses came until the early morning of January 5, at about 5:30 a.m., when I received two more. On this same day, I went into my closet to get something. There, with what I was looking for inside, I found a bag with these words written on it: "'Come, follow Me,' Jesus said, 'and I will make you fishers of men'" (Mark 1:17). I felt as if the Lord had reached down and touched me on the shoulder, for surely He had. The remainder of the poem came through my spirit during the days between January 5 and January 8. No matter what I was doing, I could "see" these words being "written" in my spirit. I would stop whatever I was doing and write them down. If it was a case where I couldn't write them down immediately, they were never forgotten.

I remembered them clearly, and I wrote them down as soon as I had the chance to put them on paper. The twenty- four verse poem "Come, Follow Me" was completed. I read the poem over and over; I could not believe what I held in my hands. I was in awe and amazement as I praised the Lord for giving me these words. I thought they were to be the last; I was wrong, for since that January of 2009, I have been given poem after poem. It has been rare when there has been a month without at least one. The majority of them, from the shortest to the longest, have been written within minutes. After the conclusion of each poem, there is at least one Scripture reference. It is my suggestion that you have a Bible available to refer to the verses. I see the poems as a "gateway" leading into the garden of the Living Word. You will be touched in just reading the poems, but they are meant to draw you further, ever closer to His heart, His heartbeat found within the pages of the Bible. Following the poems and Scriptures, you will find a short section entitled either "Background" or "Note." The "Background" is a journal of the occurrences surrounding the words, what was happening in my life or in the life of someone else when the verses were written. The section entitled "Note" is simply my personal insight into what the poem means to me. "Background" is about people in *my* life; "Note" is about how the verses touched *my* heart, *my* story, or *my* perspective—or so one might think at first.

Over the course of time that I have shared these writings with many different people and in varying situations, one thing becomes very clear. I have discovered that these verses are not limited to me, nor were they meant to be. Without a doubt, you will see your own life, dear reader, within these verses. You will recognize those who are a part of your own journey. You will feel the ebb and flow of your own emotions. In other words, these poems will be intensely *yours*. You are holding within your hands a book containing words God gave to me, words of love and encouragement that were specifically sent to *you*. They were written as an expression of His immense love for *you*. They were written for *you* to feel upon *your own* heart the touch of the Master, the Message Maker.

Dedication

This book is dedicated to my Lord and Savior, Jesus Christ.
He is the Rhyme, He is the Reason, He is the Author,
He is the Finisher, He is the Message Maker.

Acknowledgments

I have been blessed through the people God has chosen to place in my life. Were it not for each of you, these poems might have remained on my desk and been shared with a few but never reaching the possibility of being shared with so many more. I want to express my thankfulness to you, my family, friends, and church family, for all the encouragement you have given me over the course of these writings. I have even received encouragement from people I have never met, as a poem might have made its way to them through a family member or a friend. When I have heard how these hearts have been ministered to through these verses, I received renewed determination to make publishing this book my goal. Some of you will recognize yourselves in the background of a poem. I was so blessed that the Lord gave me these words to minister directly to your hearts. I am so appreciative to those who offered to take time out of their busy lives to help me compile the format for the book. Thank you to each of you. Lastly, I want to thank my grandson for helping me through the final "putting-together" stages; I am forever grateful for your love and patience, Rhandy. In compiling this acknowledgement, I sense in an even deeper way how truly blessed I am, as I have felt the touch of the Message Maker through each of you.

Contents

Biography

Leta Rae Pereira is a wife, mother, and grandmother. Born in San Jose, California, she and her husband, Joe, relocated to Hollister, California, in the spring of 2005. Within a very short time, she realized that there was a significant reason for being led to this particular place at this particular time. She found the move had been totally spiritually based, as God began opening doors she never could have imagined, and He continues to do so. She has been involved in pro-life ministry since the beginning of 2008, first serving as a volunteer counselor for Hollister Pregnancy Center and recently becoming client services director. She is also the on-staff writer for the Center. She and her husband are actively involved in their community church, Hillside Christian Fellowship. *The Message Maker* is her first book.

References

1. The Spirit-Filled Life Bible NKJV
2. The Holy Bible Authorized KJV

The words flow through my spirit
As the pen is put to paper.
I place them verse by verse,
But *He* is the Message Maker,
The Holy Spirit's Gentle Prodding
Of the words He will convey,
Words meant to reach His children
In a poem's special way.
The rhythm of rhyming thoughts,
His Heartbeat of Mercy through the lines,
The Longing of His Love
Extended throughout time.
When the lines are placed together,
When each poem is complete,
I add one to another,
Then I wait for Him to Speak,
For *all* is in *His* Timing
As to when each will be shared.
I wait here as His vessel,
For Him to Tell me when and where,
Where to carry these words He has Given.
Words to encourage, uplift, and guide,
Words to enlighten this dubious world,
Words to confirm He forever abides,
He is The Maker of each poem.
He is The Writer of each line.
He is our Heavenly Father.
His Love is yours; His Love is mine.
He Longs to Touch our hearts
In a way we will understand
That in the reading of these poems,
We will hear The Great *I AM*.

Mark 4:24

January 2011

Come, Follow Me

I heard The Voice of Jesus gently whisper to my heart,
"Come, follow Me, My child; I will be with you from the start.
Leave your cave of worldly darkness; step out into My Light.
Follow in My Footsteps as we pass through shadows of the night."

"But will the path be easy, Lord?"
My fitful flesh cried with concern.
"No, it won't," My Jesus Answered,
"For there are lessons to be learned.

"The first thing you will realize
As we walk along together
Is that this world is only temporary,
While My world is forever.

"The treasures of this world
Will never have anything to compare
With the life that I Have Given you
And the Gifts you have to share.

"The Gifts that I Have Given
Are always meant to be
An infinite Reflection
Of The Love that shines through Me.

Your Gifts flow from My Spirit
And will saturate your heart,
And as you choose to use them,
You will find yourself apart—

"Apart from those who cannot see
Or do not choose to hear,
Apart from those who choose the dark
And do not want Me near.

"You will have days of intense discouragement
And nights of deep despair.
You will grieve the loss of loved ones
And perhaps sometimes believe that I don't care.

"During these times of trial,
As you suffer these attacks,
There will be those who question you,
'Why is it that *you* lack?'

"'Where *is* this God you follow?
We thought you said your faith was true.
Where *is* this God you follow?
Has He forgotten you?'

"No, My child, The Path will not be easy;
The burdens will not be light.
The Road would seem impassable
If you journeyed with mere sight.

"But Remember, My dear child,
I, too, have Walked through this worldly life.
I have known of intense loneliness,
Of bitter sorrow, pain, and strife.

"On that hill of Calvary,
As unspeakable pain pierced through My Bones,
I searched the crowd through blood-soaked Eyes
And found Myself Alone.

"Alone, Save for the closest ones,
All My followers had fled in fear
Alone during my darkest hour
Unspeakable grief flowed through My Tears.

"My closing Eyes looked to the sky
As I hung upon that tree,
And I cried out in all My anguish,
'FATHER, WHY HAST THOU FORSAKEN ME?'

"As My tortured, pain-filled body
Exhaled its final, shuddering breath,
I whispered, 'It is finished,'
And released Myself to the appearances of death.

"Three days, those who had loved Me
Walked cloaked in distress, discouragement, and despair,
While others mocked and told them,
'Your Jesus is no longer here!

"'Where *is* this Jesus you followed?
What has happened to your King?
Where *is* this Jesus you followed?
For Him, the death toll rings!'

"But oh, the joy of morning
On that resurrection dawn
When the stone of the tomb was rolled away
AND THE KING OF KINGS WAS GONE!

"*ARISEN*!
In manifestation that my promises are true,
ARISEN! gone on to prepare a place
For my blessed loved one, *you*.

"And so, My child, I have Given you
This map for you to follow
The example of My Own Life here
In anticipation of your Eternal Tomorrow.

"And in closing, My dear child, I will leave you with these thoughts:

"The world will never know Me,
Nor the Salvation that I Brought,
If *you*, My beloved child,
Will not strive to do your part.

"You must use the Gifts I Have Given you
So that other hearts may sing
The Song of My Salvation
And know the Love I Came to bring,

"To know the reality of Eternal Life
And that my promises are true.
You see, My precious child,

"It all depends on *you*."

1 Peter 4:10
1 Corinthians 12: 4-11
1 Timothy 4:14

January 2009

There is a place deep within me
Where no one else can ever go,
Where I meet The Holy Spirit,
And He sets my heart aglow.

This Place is built of Peace profound,
Of joy beyond compare,
And when I truly seek His Face,
He always meets me there.

In times of cold and dampness,
With Winter's chill throughout my heart,
I've called upon My Master,
And He has sent warmth into each part.

In those days of deepest darkness,
When no one else could comprehend,
I've heard Him softly whisper,
"This too shall have an end."

And so, firmly planted in His Promise,
Knowing the comfort He always brings,
I've felt the barren days of Winter
Softly melt into the days of Spring.

When blossoms have bloomed with blessings
That have come forth for me to share,
As the winds of Winter's sorrow
Have been replaced with the gentle breeze of His caressing care,

Then came those days of Summer
When my soul was so parched and dry,
And the enemy had filled my mind
With discouragement built on lies.

This desert place was so torrid
I was sure my spirit would die of thirst,
But once again I heard my Jesus:
"My child, Just place Me first."

So came the day I finally said,
"Yes, Lord, I give you *all* I am,"
Fully determined to follow His Calling
In every way I can.

Reaching this place of firm decision,
I have realized within myself
That I am now in the days of Autumn,
With an overflowing abundance of Spiritual wealth.

For just as the fullness of Fall's bounty
Bursts forth in colors beyond compare,
My spirit has burst forth with its true purpose
In the realization of His Gifts that I am meant to share.

On my journey through the seasons of life's stages,
Whether I am living in shimmering sunlight or relentless rain,
My heart's foundation remains built upon The Rock of Ages,
For through Him Alone I am sustained.

Each life is touched by seasons;
There is nothing unique about mine.
Each life flows upon the river of change
That spans a course of time.

But when we look inside ourselves
To contemplate the Seasons of our days,
It is there we meet our Master,
Holding our reflection within His Gaze.

Ecclesiastes 3:1-8

March 2009

Note on "Seasons"

"Seasons" was written as I contemplated the journey of life. Just as the seasons come and go, so too do the events of our time on earth. Some changes bring hardships cold as winter. Others bring joy bright as summer sunshine. As we draw closer to Him, He awakens in us the gifts we have been given and are meant to share. It is then our spirit bursts into "colors" as glorious as autumn. But there is one circumstance that is, has always been, and forever will be unchanging: the unconditional love that God has for each of us. It is there always, throughout the fluctuating circumstances of our lives. He waits, holding the unchangeable within His hands.

Forgiveness

Father, It's happened once again.
When will this ever end?
My emotions at another crossroads;
Do I have to choose forgiveness?

Weapons of words come out of nowhere
To swiftly pierce their mark,
The so-newly healed wounds
Of an already shattered heart.

Do I have to choose forgiveness?

People I have trusted
As being a true reflection of who You are
Have had Your Light evaporate around them,
As a cloudy night obliterates a sky of stars.

Do I have to choose forgiveness?

I have found myself under judgment by others,
My intentions so misunderstood.
They have seen my decisions as unworthy
When I know they have only been meant for the good.

Do I have to choose forgiveness?

As I contemplate this question
That incessantly hammers at the door of my soul,
Jesus has come to Answer,
And the following He has told:

"My child, You ask where you can find this forgiveness?

"In your flesh, it is so hard to see.
That's because, My Dear Child,
It doesn't exist there.
It can only be found through Me.

"If you truly follow Me,
Then In forgiveness there is *no* choice.
You have already heard My Answer
When you have listened for My Voice.

"I Am unconditional love;
Through My Spirit forgiveness flows.
Those who truly seek me
Are those who fully know.

"Unforgiveness is destruction
Of the Spirit meant to be
An ever-flowing fountain of unconditional love,
The Love that comes from Me.

"As tools designed for torture
Ripped My Flesh and Bones asunder,
My Spirit cried out, '*FORGIVE THEM, FATHER*,'
For the deception they are under.

"The measure of My Forgiveness
Can be found within the span
Of My tattered Arms outstretched upon The Cross,
Held open by nail-pierced Hands.

"So You see, My Child,

"When you contemplate My Sacrifice,
It is then you will know what is true.
You have no choice in forgiveness;
You are meant to forgive
The way *I* have Forgiven you.

Ephesians 4:32

May 2009

Background of "Forgiveness"

I had been devastated by the news of a very public accusation (a very serious accusation) that was made against someone I have known for a few years now, someone well respected in the Christian community who seemed to be doing everything possible to follow The Lord, which made the fall seem all that much further. Though not a minister or church leader ,his work placed him in a position to be watched by many as he lived out his Christian walk. Though this didn't involve me personally, I still felt a deep sense of betrayal for myself as well as all others who knew and trusted this person. The question that kept rotating through my spirit was, how can I forgive? The Lord gave me the answer in the early hours of one morning with the beginning lines of the poem "Forgiveness."

He re-opened my eyes to the fact that striving to live life in the Spirit while still in the flesh is difficult, to say the least, for all of us. ("The spirit is willing, but the flesh is weak.") He reminded me that if I found myself losing *my* perspective that I could also easily be on a downward spiral. I had no right to harbor a sense of regret and unforgiveness. What was meant to be rooted in my spirit was mercy and forgiveness, not judgment. It's not that I haven't known this is how it's supposed to be; it's just that it had been easier to think about it as something that would be easy for me to do. It's always easy to "think;" it's the "doing" that's hard—but I know it's possible. My prayer is that this poem will touch many hearts with the *full* realization of the *magnitude* of *forgiveness* and what it is meant to be, as seen through the eyes of Jesus as He hung from the Cross.

The Eleventh Hour

In the early morning hours,
My spirit crying with despair,
During these hours of deepest darkness,
I whisper, "Jesus, Are You here?"

But there is no answer.

The shadows of the night
Slowly slip into the dawn.
I pray, "Jesus, with one Touch from You,
My fears will all be gone."

But there is no answer.

The misty hours of morning
Tick their minutes throughout time.
"Jesus, You've seen others' problems;
Why can You not See mine?"

But there is no answer.

Noontime has arrived,
With the sun so high above.
My spirit continues to question,
"Jesus, Have You taken from me Your Love?"

But there is no answer.

The hours of the afternoon
Stretch out along their way.
My heart beats more frantically.
"Jesus, Will there be no release from my dilemma today?"

But there is no answer.

As the color of a deep-blue sky
Gives way to the afterglow of day,
My downtrodden spirit queries,
"Jesus, Is there nothing You will Say?"

But there is no answer.

The darkness of this night
Seems deeper than the one before.
My spirit has no more strength as I cry out,
"My Jesus, I can't take this anxiety anymore!"

But there is no answer.

As midnight time approaches
And I relentlessly meditate on my plight,
I know the eleventh hour has come;
It will soon be too late for anything to turn out right.

Then *suddenly*, As a storm-tossed ship
On a pitch-black sea sights the shore from a lighthouse beacon,
My soul is flooded with brilliant Light
And The Peace I have been seeking.

Is it because circumstances have changed
That I find my heart so relieved?
No, Circumstances are still the same.
The difference is I now *realize* I have been deceived.

Deceived into thinking that I walk alone,
That The One Who Created me doesn't care.
Deceived into thinking that all has been lost
And that my situation in life isn't fair.

For as my mind turns the pages
Through my life's past stages,
Only then is it that I can recall
And only then can I hear *His* Voice above all.

"My Child,

"How many times, In your eleventh hour,
Have I proven My Promise is true?
How many times have you seen My Hand move
When you had thought there was nothing I would do?

"Faith is not Faith until it is *all* you have left,
When there seems nothing positive in anything you see.
When you come to the end of yourself, releasing your doubt,
You find the essence of faith is in Me.

"Your eleventh hour miracle
Will be a manifestation of My Glory,
For the Spiritual Eyes of others will be opened
Through the unfolding of your life's story.

"Your eleventh hour miracle
May not look like what you have planned.
No matter what circumstances seem,
Remember who I Am.

"My Dear Child,

"When you call upon My Name in your hour of deepest need,
Do not look for an answer to come,
For *I Am The Answer*;
The victory has already been won.

Isaiah 42:16

June 2009

Background of "The Eleventh Hour"

I had been speaking with someone who was facing a very difficult situation, something she would have never imagined she would have to go through. As this person told me about her fears she said, "When I come into times like these, I always think about what you've told me about the eleventh hour and how miracles can happen, and then I don't lose faith." Two days after this conversation, at about 5:30 a.m., I awoke with the start of this poem in my spirit. I believe "The Eleventh Hour" is the Lord's response to the person I was speaking with, a response to her cry, a response to *all* of our cries. Whatever and whenever they may be, His Expression of assurance is that He is *always present,* no matter what the hour.

I have reached a very special place
From where I never plan to return.
The journey here has taken years,
Over paths paved with lessons learned.

As a train winds its way through a valley
To begin its mountaintop ascent,
So my life has wound through twists and turns
During these days on earth I have spent.

My mind meanders back through time
To contemplate where this journey had its start.
I can still see the place with crystal-clarity.
I remember It started right here, Within my heart.

When a little girl of six years old
Sat staring at a star-studded sky,
Watching, wondering, whispering,
Sobbing the question, Why?

"Why is there so much sadness?"
"Why can't we all live in love?"
"Is there Someone up there behind those stars?"
"Are You really there, God, high above?"

I felt The Heart of Jesus break
As He listened to my cries.
I felt His Arms reach to surround me
From the expanse of that night sky.

And I *knew* …

That as the love of a true parent
Intertwines with their child's heart,
I knew Jesus was my Father,
And we would never be apart.

Time ticked on, swiftly slipping away
Through the ups and downs of living,
Until one day I realized
How little I had been giving.

I had neglected to give back To My Faithful Father, My Friend.
I had forgotten what His Love was all about.
So centered was I deep within myself,
Filled with insecurities, frustrations, self-doubt.

But He brought me to remembrance…

For here I rest in that special place
That was spoken of as this poem began.
After "stilling myself" and releasing my doubts,
I have now come to remember who I am.

I am nothing in myself.
I am dust upon the wind,
For the life I have been given
Has *always* belonged to *Him*.

In recent days I've found my thoughts
Returning back to that night filled with Heaven's glow
When a little girl looked into a star covered sky,
Her spirit seeking, Searching to know.

The Arms that Gave me shelter
Drawing me to The Father I came to know
Were truly The Everlasting Arms,
For They have *never* let me go.

He Held me close and assured me
Of who I was meant to be   :
The reflection of My Father
For all the world to see.

The Light of the Holy Spirit
Burns bright inside of me
As I hear The Gentle Voice of Jesus say,
"My Child, The Truth has set you free."

Psalm 31

August 2009

Background of "Remembering"

"Remembering" is a poem that reflects my life. I am the little girl within the lines, yet I know that there are so many others who will recognize themselves within these verses, so it belongs to each of us. It is a testimony to the never-ending steadfastness of the Father's love and faithfulness. Though we may forget in the busyness of our days, His plan and purpose for our lives, His patience with us is never-ending. He waits for us to remember back to the times when His love carried us, to remember that He carries us still and to realize that He always will.

When I contemplate compassion,
The first thing my spirit sees
Are the Gentle Eyes of Jesus
Softly gazing back at me.

I hear His Voice speak quietly
From the depths within my heart
And know with full awareness
The message He pleads to impart:

"My child,

"There are so many of my children
Crying out for a loving touch or word.
I Know that you have seen their plight,
But it seems you have not fully heard.

"When you said that you would follow Me,
You gave your life away
To let My Presence work through you
In all things day to day.

"I now depend on you to show
My Love in everything you can,
For only in this way will others come to know
The *essence* of Who I Am."

My righteous reply is swift:

"But Father, I don't always have an opportunity
To do what You have asked,
For I don't meet someone in need daily
Who happens to cross *my* path."

My observation meets with Silence
As He waits for me to realize
That the way that I have seen things
Has not been through His Eyes.

"My child, Do you remember
The father whose only child is living her last days upon this earth?
Were you to offer a loving word to him,
How much would it be worth?

"Or the woman who is suffering
As she endures her family's trials—
A sick child, a lack of money—
Could you talk with her awhile?

"Or the young girl tormented
By the decision she had made
To abort her unborn child?
Her endless sadness does not fade.

"Have you looked within your family
To find the pain within their hearts?
Is there something you could do or say
That would in *their* healing have a part?

"The person in the grocery line
With weariness etched into her face,
What would a smile mean to her ?
Would she sense My Presence in that place?

"You see, My child,
In your perceptions you have been deceived,
For everywhere you look, daily
You will find someone in need.

"Good intentions without actions
Mean nothing in My Sight.
If you are truly My disciple,
You will lead others to My Light.

"In My heavenly garden,
The rose of compassion stands apart,
For its beauty is a Reflection
Of The Love that is My Heart.

"Please take this rose and share it
With *everyone* you meet,
For it is then you will be My true vessel,
And it is then that you will find yourself complete.

Matthew 25:34–40

November 2009

Note on "Compassion"

As I wrote this poem, I had a vision of the Lord's heart, the very center, where compassion resides. His compassion is expressed through arms that open wide in outreach, to sight that goes beyond focusing on ourselves in a mirror, to feelings that go beyond what's happening inside ourselves. When we have eyes like His, we think about and respond to the needs of others. In doing so, we find our own burdens become easier to bear, as we realize that He is Carrying *our* load for us.

The Unending Story

Each life has a story all its own
That begins with the body's first breath.
Thoughts shadowed in sadness believe the story is finished
Upon the last breath exhaled at death.

But The Author of each book of life,
Who has Lovingly Written each line,
Gently opens the eyes of our spirit
To an awareness that we are surrounded by signs.

For when we truly contemplate
The arrangement of His Creation,
We realize that death is *not* the end.
Rather, it is a magnificent transformation.

For does He not Turn dark into light?
Night into day?
Winter into Springtime?
The setting sun of a sunset into a rising sun with brilliant rays?

There is nothing of destruction
In our Loving Creator's Plan.
If we see it throughout Nature,
Why can we not see it in the life of man?

Dark flows into light,
Night flows into day,
Death flows into life,
There is just no other way.

His Heart flows with Compassion
For those left behind in sorrow,
And so He gives His Promise:
We will one day share in an Eternal tomorrow.

And on that glorious day
When we are joined with our loved ones once again,
We will know without a doubt
The story of a life is a story without an end.

John 3:16

January 2010

Background of "The Unending Story"

The mother of a friend of mine passed away, and my friend asked if I could write a poem for her memorial service. I prayed for the Lord's direction, and "The Unending Story" was the result. I have always felt that this particular poem is written for those who have not yet been touched by a close walk with the Lord; they may believe in God but not actually realize how close He is to each of us. As I read the poem at the service, I could strongly sense the Lord opening the doors of the hearts present. One lady came up to me afterward and said, "Honey, I don't do church, but that poem really touched me." Her husband had recently passed away, and she had tears in her eyes as she spoke. I know it was Jesus Who touched her that day, pouring His peace and comfort over her in a way she had never experienced. My prayer is that she went on to read The Words of John 3:16 , and that she took His Hand as He held it out to her.

To Surrender

To sense The Power of Your Presence, Lord,
To live within Your Light,
To do the things from day to day
That are precious in Your Sight,

To have The Power of Your Anointing
Fall in flames of fire from above,
To fill each and every space in me
With Your Redeeming Love,

To know Your Will in all I do,
To trust without a doubt
That Your Voice that prompts within me
Will manifest Your Will without,

To capture the capacity
To grasp Your Grace from others,
To see each as we truly are
As sisters and as brothers,

To array in Armor daily,
To walk within Your Will,
To be an empty vessel,
To be with Your Purpose filled,

To be lifted to a higher place,
To contemplate the "Essence" of the earth,
To see with eyes of full awareness,
To know in You life finds its worth,

To see it is not for me to ponder,
To know the "perfect" time,
To take a step outside myself,
To ask "Lord, Is this Your Sign?"

To know Your Will is Perfect,
To recognize Your Guidance as *always* true,
To bring me to surrender,
To find myself in You.

Matthew 16:25

January 2010

Note on "To Surrender"

To surrender. This was the decision that changed my life forever, lifting me to heights I had never imagined.. When I finally said, "Yes, Lord, I place *You* first. I surrender *my* life to *You*." In that moment, a door was opened for Him to work miracles, and they were manifesting in *my* life. It is my heart's desire that you, too, dear reader, come to that point of surrender. For when you do, you will realize that you have lost nothing but gained more than you *ever* could have fathomed. You will *know* your life's purpose as you, too, begin to soar on the wings of His love.

"Peace I leave with you;
Do not be afraid."
These are the Words of Jesus;
This is The Promise that He made.

In the world you will have tribulation;
This is very plain to see.
In spite of *any* circumstance,
Keep your eyes on Me.

My Peace is Supernatural;
Something the world does not understand.
Those apart cannot know My Comfort,
For they do not know Who I Am.

But *you*, My Child, are My Own.
I Called you before your body's first breath.
In Me you have fullness of Life,
While those in the world can see only death.

My Peace will flow like a River
Over the turmoil in your soul.
Call upon Me in your darkness;
You will once again be made whole.

Call upon Me in every moment,
For My Peace is meant to be
The essence of your entire life,
Built upon the Foundation you have in Me.

When situations become overwhelming
And life seems to make no sense,
Remember The Words that I have left with you
And ponder what they have meant.

I Am the Prince of Peace;
I Am the Source of all days.
I Am the Alpha and the Omega;
I Am the only way.

Perhaps when others see your Peace
They may ask you to explain.
You will then be their Living Light to Me,
And another soul for Heaven will be gained.

Then, When your final moment on earth arrives
And your life here has been done,
You will *see* Me as your Bridge
To your Eternity of Peace to come.

John 14:27

February 2010

Note on "The Bridge of Peace"

Peace: the Lord's heartfelt *desire* for *each* of us. Fear, anxiety, worry, these are not of Him. He longs for us to find that *center* where we find *complete rest*. Like a child afraid of the dark, calling out for his father's protection, we have only to call upon Jesus. He *will* come, and where He is, turmoil cannot exist, only Peace. He is our Bridge, our connection, extending peace inside this life and outward into eternity.

Dear Jesus, I come to You this morning
Upon a wave of endless praise,
For Your Mercy is Eternal,
And it is Your Love that fills my days.

As I kneel before You in prayer,
Overwhelmed by Your Power and Might,
These lines within my spirit unfold;
These words I begin to write.

When the sunshine of serenity is reflected
Over the sea of my life's story,
My heart is filled with happiness;
My spirit sings of Your Glory.

Then *suddenly*, from seemingly nowhere,
Clouds of deepest darkness come.
The waves begin to crash and surge;
My soul screams, "You *must* run!"

The enemy's wicked whisper
Begins ringing in my ears:
"You must flee while you still have time;
Go far away from here!

"Run to where the streams are smooth,
Where days flow one by one.
Think about yourself…if you should stay.
Think about the greater storms that will surely come.

"Change the course of your wayward journey.
You were not meant to go.
Return to solid ground
And to that comfortable place you've always known."

My response is *firm* and *final*;
I was ready to tell him from the start:
"NO, devil of deception,
You will have NO PLACE within THIS HEART!"

In earlier days of life,
When the tempest around me lashed,
I would have surely fled,
But those days are now long past.

Now you are defeated, Satan;
I see through all your lies,
For The Father of Eternity
Has His Hand upon my eyes.

Now I have *fully* sought *JESUS* for my direction,
And it is He Who holds my hand
As we stand inside my storm-tossed ship
And move far away from land.

For as I write these verses,
Is there above me a cloudless sky?
No, The wild wind is wailing;
The unknown all around me lies.

The battle rages in the heavenlies
As the warring angels clash.
I hear the clanging of their swords;
I feel the "breath" of each sword's slash.

The Light of Heaven is drawing closer;
The Power of Prayer has had its way.
The darkness is dispelling;
We will soon see the Dawn of a new Day.

The Precious Blood of The Lamb
Has been my protection through it all.
Within the hurricane, He *hears* my cries;
He *answers* my *every* call.

He has been my Faithful Father and Friend
Through *all* I have ever borne,
And so I will ever rejoice in Him
As I praise Him in this and in *every* storm.

Isaiah 25:4–5

April 2010

Note on "Everlasting Praise"

When things are going well and our lives seem to be comparatively in order, praise flows easily. We are thankful, sitting upon our comfortable cushion of trouble-free circumstances. But when the tempest rages around us, when sobs of grief threaten to choke us, when we are so fatigued from struggle that we feel we have no more strength to speak, and when the darkness is so deep around us that we can no longer see where we are going, praise becomes an almost unimaginable thing to do. Yet, it is *this* very praise that comes out of pain that brings the *greatest victory*. It is the *praise* in strife that will carry us *through* the storms, as we walk with the Prince of Peace through all conditions.

Transformation

"Life is what you make it,"
I have often heard it said,
In songs that I have heard sung
And in books that I have read.

But as my walk with Jesus
Has grown closer day by day,
I've come to see these words
In a completely different way.

For as I have surrendered
To the Loving Guidance of His Hand,
I see my life's true purpose unfold
Through the manifestation of His Plan.

The meaning of my life
Is now so much more profound,
For in The Rock of Ages
I am standing on *solid ground.*

Where before my emotions changed
Like the ebb and flow of tides,
I have now found true stability
With Jesus by my side.

He has led me down paths
Where I thought I would never tread.
When I once would have been fearful,
I now have unshakeable confidence in what He has said.

"I will never leave you nor forsake you,"
I found so clearly said within His Word.
It was there for me to plainly see,
But I had never truly heard.

My restless spirit had been searching,
So dry and parched with thirst,
Until the moment I finally said,
"Lord, I place You first."

In that one decision
I turned my life over to Him.
Now What *He* wants shines with so much brilliance
While what *I* want has grown so dim.

Now I know the true meaning of my life
Could never come from me—
That was an illusion—
But The Truth has set me free.

In the places of greatest happiness
Or in the depths of deepest grief,
I can now say, "*Thy Will be done*,"
Resting inside His Indescribable Peace.

His Faithfulness is endless;
His Promises are true.
What He has done for me,
He will *surely* do for you.

Then the words "Life is what you make it"
Won't have the same meaning anymore.
You, too, will find He Alone is The Creator of *your* life,
And it is *Him* you are living for.

Romans 12:2

November 2009

Note on "Transformation"

I was comfortable with myself for many years, thinking I was handling my life well, taking care of a family, working in a business, doing all the day-to-day things it takes to run a home. I was comfortable with myself until I realized I hadn't really known who I was at all. I was living life "on the surface." I had not yet touched the depth of my being, where the true meaning of life resides, that depth where I could hear His voice, His guidance, where I could realize that my worth is only found *in Him,* not in anything I could do or be. I was living in a cocoon of self-reliance, a caterpillar that doesn't know it's a butterfly until it's been transformed.

My Jesus, As I stop to contemplate
The years upon this earth You spent,
My thoughts are drawn to Your mother, Mary,
And what her relationship with You had meant.

As she cradled You in her arms
On that early Christmas morn,
Could she have ever fully comprehended
The reason for which You had been born?

When she gazed upon Your Infant Face,
As she looked down through the years,
Could her then joy-filled heart ever fathom
A heart that would one day hold an ocean of her tears?

As she ran to hold and comfort You,
When her little boy stumbled and fell at play,
Could she ever have envisioned, as she nursed Your scarred knees,
That You would fall beneath the weight of a cross some day?

When You began Your Ministry,
Did her mother's heart scream out *NO*?
Could she have then already known deep within her being
Where on Your journey You would go?

On that road to Calvary,
As she stood so utterly helpless and yet so nearby,
How could she see her beloved Son beaten and tortured?
Her own cries of agony must have filled the sky.

When she saw Your tattered Body
Hanging upon that tree,
Could she have screamed out to Heaven,
Asking to be blinded, so as not to see?

During the three days that must have seemed Eternity
Between Good Friday and Easter's Dawn,
Could she have despairingly questioned Your Promise to return,
Buried in the grief that You might be forever gone?

Her struggle must have been incomprehensible,
As she had nothing left, only the seeds of her faith.
How could she have seen, in those darkest of days,
That her Son would soon unlock Heaven's Gates?

Oh, But *then*, When the sunrise of the Resurrection
Burst The Light of Your Love into that first Easter day,
How could she have *ever* stopped *rejoicing*,
Blessed with the assurance her Son would forever be the way?

And so, my Jesus, As I think about Your Mother
And all that she endured,
I remember Your Resurrection
And realize that *every* mother's heart is in Your Love secure.

For *every* mother is precious to You,
Just as precious as Your Own,
And each that has planted seeds of Faith
Will one day see the great harvest she has sown.

Our children *will* come to fully know You,
To walk with You day by day.
And then they will realize, without a doubt
What we, their mothers, have been trying to say.

You were, You are, and You forever will be The Way.

John 14:6

May 2010

Background of "Memories of Mother Mary"

A close friend was in deep sadness over the paths her children had chosen to walk. Yet, despite what circumstances may seem, she still clings to a promise given to her years ago that *all* of her children will one day come to serve the Lord. I know the Lord gave me this poem for her, as well as for all mothers everywhere who wait upon Him to draw their children into His flock. Through the verses, He is saying, "My child, see what My own mother endured while upon this earth. See how sadness was transformed into eternal joy; there will be no less for you.

Living Praise

Lord, What is the essence of Praise?
How can it be put into words?
Is it held within the songs that we sing?
Or is it a song we have never truly heard?

We strive to hear Your Answer, Lord,
To know what pleases You.
Is there a special song You would Love to Hear?
For You, There is nothing we would not do.

"My child,

"Praise is more than mouthing words
Of an often-sung Church hymn.
Praise is thunder erupting in your heart
Until all other sounds grow dim.

"Thunder that precedes the storm,
A Spiritual Wind of hurricane force,
The darkness is growing darker;
Your purpose *must* increase in strength to stay the course.

"Praise is taking the songs that you sing
And walking the words into your living.
Praise streams to My Throne through song
When it flows through the love that you are giving.

"You may offer Sunday songs to Me
In music filled with beautiful words,
But Praise must be brought into your actions;
My Voice have you not yet heard?

"When I Open doors within your life,
Do not be afraid to walk through.
Lean on me, believe in me, trust in me,
Praise Me for all I can and will do.

"My Heart *longs* for you to Praise Me
Not only in song But in words and deed.
Singing songs without works is fruitless.
Can you expect a harvest without planting seed?

"So as you sing these songs today,
I Cherish every voice.
But remember, the songs go further
And each of you has a choice,

"A choice to take the songs you sing
And carry them inside your heart.
Carry them out into a dying world
As you set yourselves apart.

"I Am not Asking for perfection;
All I Ask is that you try
To set your life to The Music of My Heart
So that others may see Me through your eyes.

"For in the end,

"The greatest hymn of Praise
Is the *life* that is a song.
The day-to-day things said and done,
This is The Praise and Worship for which I long.

Hebrews 13:15-16

July 2010

Background of "Living Praise"

One night at Bible study, I said that the Lord had given me a poem that morning. Though I was anxious to share it, I knew He was telling me to wait, and He confirmed why the next day. The next morning, one more verse was added, this particular verse coming with a sense of insistency and urgency:

> *When I Open doors within your life,*
> *Do not be afraid to walk through.*
> *Lean on Me, believe in Me, trust in Me,*
> *Praise Me for all I can and will do.*

In talking with a woman in the church later, the Lord gave me *total* confirmation of how important these words were. (The woman had no idea what was in this poem, as I had not yet shared it.) She was telling me how she and her family *knew* the Lord was opening a door in their lives for change, but they had hesitancy and fear to go through it. At the same time, they knew that if they didn't take the step forward, a tremendous God-given opportunity would be lost. So they had made their choice to *stand* on His promise of faithfulness and provision. *Moving ahead, they were doing exactly what the verse says :leaning on Him, believing in Him, trusting in Him.* The highest form of praise was being offered, as they praised Him for circumstances yet unseen.

Through this woman's description of her circumstances to me, the Lord truly gave me a picture to go with the verse of this poem. This family was putting His promises into living praise, and they would be richly rewarded. Many of us are being given opportunities to walk through doors that the Lord is holding open for us, opportunities for a new direction, new ministries, new ways to reach out to our communities, *ways to demonstrate His promise of faithfulness at work in our lives.* I know the sense of insistency and urgency is because, in these end times, our testimonies to His faithfulness are *priceless* to Him, for what is it but our testimony worked through His power that will save the lost? Too many times, we tend to psychoanalyze, tear apart, and question actions we were destined to take. We question because we fear, and when we fear too long, the door closes; an opportunity is missed, a testimony is lost, revival is smoldered, and praise that could have been offered lies in ashes at the feet of complacency.

Next time we begin to sing our praises to Him, let us *especially* praise Him for the "opening doors" and the strength He will *surely* give us to walk through them, for we were *made* to worship Him in *all* we do.

His Kingdom Comes

Sing a new song of Glory
To The Everlasting King;
Let all Creation bow
As the sound of Praises ring.

Faith that has been tarnished
Will be burnished to pure gold.
All the things which I Have Promised
Have now begun to happen as foretold.

Mighty mountains of obstruction
That have blocked your way to Me
Are crumbling into piles
That will slip into the sea.

I Have Heard My Faithful crying
In the deepest dark of night.
Prince of Deception, your time is nigh;
You will soon be blinded by My Light

My Heart has Cried enough
For the suffering I Have Seen,
Families ripped asunder
As all things become unclean.

Those who use My Name
To satisfy their endless gluttonous greed,
These will see the full fire of My Wrath,
As too late they will plead.

My Precious little children tortured,
Their innocence stripped away,
Those who abuse and use them
Are destined in an eternity of hell to stay.

My Creation filled with beauty
Buried under a canopy of evil,
Demonic entities running rampant
As anything of goodness they try to steal.

My truly Faithful Followers,
It is now time to reveal:
I Have Seen your heartfelt purpose
As before My Throne you kneel.

The façade of hypocrisy
Will soon be ripped away
As the Host of Heaven's Realm
Prepares for the Dawn of a new day.

Signs and Wonders will be seen
As never before upon this earth.
Sleeping eyes will be awakened
As the sword slashes Satan's curse.

As the crash of coming conflict
Grows closer with each day,
Fear not, My child,
For I Will *Forever* Lead The Way.

Though others see total darkness,
You will always see My Light.
This is what will guide you
As I Keep you in My Sight.

My warring Angels are gathering
As the trumpet call draws near.
This is no time for slumber;
Keep your ears attuned to hear.

Take every opportunity
I Shall Give you in these days
To take My Message to the lost,
That *many* souls be saved.

I Am The Lamb Who was slain,
My Blood shed for each one.
The fulfillment of My Promise is near,
That you shall see My Kingdom Come.

Revelation 5:9–13

July 2010

Background of "His Kingdom Comes"

Just as I was getting off the freeway on my way to my daughter's house one morning, I heard these words in my spirit: "Sing a new song." When I got to her house, I wrote down the first verse of the poem, which reads:

Sing a new Song of Glory
To The Everlasting King.
Let all Creation bow
As the sound of Praises ring.

Right after I wrote this first verse, I opened my Bible to reread Revelation 4:1–3, which Pastor had talked about the previous Sunday. But the Lord had *more* for me to read. As I saw the words in Revelation 5:9 stand out clearly, it was as if He was running a highlighter across my heart. As I read the words "and they sang a new song," *immediately* the poem began to flow.

Within minutes, it was complete. Following is the result, the coming intensifying conflict between good and evil, in which Jesus will reign victorious *forevermore.*

Note

Before writing this poem, I had *never* been drawn to the book of Revelation. Truthfully, I had always been afraid to read it; I had always said, "I'd really rather not know what's coming, Lord!" But this poem has totally changed my perspective. The minute I had finished writing the last word, I felt I had walked *very* close to heaven's gate. Where I had fear, I now had a thirst to enter into Revelation, as the Lord had gently drawn me out of my comfort zone once again. I could hear Him saying, "You will not only read the book of Revelation, you will study it in depth." And my response was, "I'm okay with that now, Lord, because of Your amazing grace. I'm *ready* to "sing a new song."

Revelation continues ...

This poem draws much more deeply into the book of Revelation than I had ever realized. It was only once I really began my study that I was able to see how many of the verses actually correspond to specific Scriptures within the first chapters. I counted fifteen references within the poem. Based on the fact that I have *never* even read Revelation prior to writing this poem, this is one more confirmation that *God is speaking* and that we *must* "keep our ears attuned to hear."

As I contemplated what it means
To reach out in His Name,
The Lord Gave me these verses;
Flowing through my spirit, the following came:

If you are looking for a breakthrough
In the strife you have in living,
Take your eyes off of yourself
And focus them on giving.

Though your wallet may be empty
And your table nearly bare,
You hold a treasure deep within you
That has been waiting to be shared.

The treasure that you have held
Is more precious than pure gold.
It has no source within this world,
And it cannot be bought or sold.

It flows from the depth of Spirit,
Where pure Love has its start.
Its birth comes through the Compassion
That streams from My Own Heart.

What do you have of value
That you can offer from this place?
Many things you hold there,
And all are a Reflection of My Grace.

Your life was meant for outreach,
Not to be curled up within yourself.
The tools I Have lain within *your* heart
Are meant to minister to *someone else.*

You have speech to offer strength;
You have hands to help with tasks;
You have feet to reach others in need,
Though for help they have not asked.

You have arms to offer comfort;
You have experiences lived to teach;
You have a smile to light someone's darkness,
When happiness for them seems so out of reach.

You are ready to help your family;
You are always there for your friends;
Yet when you minister to a stranger,
You share the Love that I intend.

On that Glorious Day
When you shall meet Me Face to face,
We will speak about the deeds
That you have done while in this place.

Did you live from the inside out,
From The Brilliance of My Light?
Or were your eyes strained upon yourself
As you stumbled through this world's night?

Did you do all for My Glory,
So that others came to know Who I Am?
Did you carry The Light of My Presence
As your actions painted a picture of The Lamb?

If you have fully understood
The reason why I Came,
Then you have walked as My disciple;
You have lived your life the same.

These words belong in times to come,
But what of now, today?
Your concern right now is for yourself
As you try to find your way.

Yet remember:

In searching for a release
From all you are going through,
You must first reach out to others,
The way I always reach out to you

Matthew 25:31–40

September 2010

Note on "Inside Out"

We cry out to the Lord, and we wonder why no help seems to come. We wonder why we have no joy, no peace, no comfort. This poem points us in the direction of *where* all of these can be found. For when we consider the question, "What is our purpose in being alive?" it is then we come to the answer. It is to serve, to reach out; it has nothing to do with inward focus. When we forget about ourselves and minister to others, it opens the door wide for Jesus to come in and minister to *us,* holding our joy, our peace, and our comfort within His hands.

Introspection

My Child,

You cry out to Me in prayer;
You seek Me in My Word.
You praise Me in your worship,
Yet My Voice you have not heard.

You pick and choose what suits you
On this "walk" you have with Me,
But the path you walk is aimless;
Your sight is too blind to see.

You are looking for an answer
For the turmoil in your life.
You ask, "Where is the joy that was promised?"
When all you see is strife.

My Child,

You cannot have a harvest
From a field that has not been sown.
You cannot expect My Faithfulness
When the Love I Ask for has not been shown.

I Am *not* a God of compromise;
I Am a God of Truth.
Do you truly live for Me?
Your actions are My proof.

You may know My Scriptures Word for Word;
You may sing such beautiful songs.
You may do these all sincerely,
But where is the manifestation of Love for which I Long?

Where is My Love that you are preaching?
Where is My Living Word that you are teaching?
Where are you sharing My Name with others?
Through you, Where has My Heart been Reaching?

I Have Said so many times
That you must place Me first;
There is no other way
That will satisfy your thirst.

So if you really long for Me,
In this moment make the choice
To keep your eyes on Heaven,
For only then will you clearly hear My Voice.

1 Corinthians 13:2
James 2:24–26

September 2010

Note on "Introspection"

We cannot walk with one foot in the world and the other in God's kingdom. A flock of sheep cannot go in two different directions; they are only able to follow *one* shepherd. For a farmer to produce a crop, he must first do the work of planting the seeds. Seeds merely sprinkled on the ground will produce nothing, just as words without actions will manifest only barrenness.

Our lives are a reflection of our love for Him. The mirror of heaven sees clearly; there are no shadows in it.

When I awoke this morning,
My heart was filled with Living Light,
For My Savior had walked with me
Through the shadows of the night.

On the other side of darkness,
There will *always* be The Son.
His Name is Jesus Christ;
The victory He Has Won.

Through *every* valley I have crossed,
Over *every* mountain I have climbed,
Have I *ever* gone alone?
NO, there has never been a time.

His Faithfulness is constant--
As the recurring of the seasons.
His Love is never ending.
For fear there is no reason.

I have felt His Profound Presence
In the first cry of a baby's breath.
I have heard His Gentle Voice calling loved ones
At the moment of their death.

From the doorway of earth's entrance
To our arrival at Heaven's Gate,
His River of Mercy flows continually
Over all things, small and great.

His Faithfulness is forever,
Though at times His Voice seems Stilled.
He Will Not Push or Pressure;
He Quietly Waits for us to do His Will.

When the storms of life are raging
And I feel all is lost,
I stop and think of The Cross on Calvary;
I ponder how much that Sacrifice cost.

If I had hung upon a cross
To show the endless depth of my caring,
Would I ever leave my loved one's side?
Could I ever not share in the pain that they are bearing?

The cost He Paid was beyond measure;
For us, There was *nothing else* He Could Do.
Did Calvary paint a picture of His endless Love?
I will leave YOUR answer up to YOU.

John 3:16

October 2010

Note on "The Question at The Cross"

Jesus, the Lamb Who was slain, our Lord and Savior. Do we truly know how much we owe to Him? If He had chosen *not* to come to earth, if He had chosen *not* to suffer and die for each of us, our lives would end with our last breath here . Instead, He chose *to* come; He chose *to* suffer and die an agonizing death in order that we might live on into Eternity with Him.

Lord,

When I listen for Your Voice,
Yet all becomes so still.
I have to ask the question,
Am I walking in Your Will?

When instead of profound Peace
Waves in my spirit roll in deepest doubt,
And I fear, Will it *ever* again be possible
To manifest Your Will without?

When my flesh cries, "Lord, I'm happy here!"
I could stay and be content.
I hear Your Gentle Whisper:
"My Child, When I Said, 'Come follow Me,'
This is *not* what I have Meant.

"Though I Have Led you for a moment
To a place you have come to know,
You *must not* hesitate
When you hear My Voice Say *go*.

"You must put the past behind you,
For all here has been said and done.
The message has been given;
I now Say to you, '*Come.*'

"You have been planted in this place
To stay but for a season.
For you to now remain
There is no further reason.

"These people you have come to love
Will always be your sisters and your brothers,
But when you choose to place Me First,
You cannot look to others.

"Do not look to others
For what you can only find in Me.
Follow My direction,
For only then will you truly *see*.

"My Plan includes your family;
It is not meant for only you.
Take your eyes off of yourself
And see what I Will Do.

"You must continue on this journey
Where you have heard my call.
Do not be overcome by flesh,
For in flesh is accomplished *nothing* at all.

"And there is much to be accomplished
In these last and final days.
This is no time for hesitation;
You must continue on my way.

"The price of disobedience
Is much too high to pay,
For if you choose denial,
In My Will you cannot stay.

"Remember, My Dear Child,
I have Called you as My Own.
You should have no further doubts
Through all that I Have Shown.

"As *all* is in My Timing,
So this, too, has its place.
Keep your eyes upon this moment,
And see The Reflection of My Face.

"Carry it with you to other places,
Wherever I May Lead.
Carry it with you to the lost
As you continue planting seed.

"Then, When your feet follow in My Footsteps
And all becomes so still,
You will once again hear My Voice with clarity,
For it is then you will be walking in My Will."

Psalm 32:8

October 2010

Background of "Walking in His Will"

I had been trying to stifle the promptings of the Lord to leave a church where I had grown very comfortable. I loved all the people there, and I was involved in praise and worship; it felt like family. It felt like the perfect place to be. But the Lord was telling me it wasn't, that I needed to leave. I had just chosen not to hear, until one Saturday when He gave me this poem. The very next morning at church, a word was spoken over me. The word was: "God says to get your running shoes on; you are going to be on the move." No one knew about the poem. With tears streaming down my face and onto the song sheets, I put away the praise and worship music I had so enjoyed singing. I went in to see the pastor and gave him a copy of this poem.

As soon as I closed the door behind me, I felt as if an immense burden had been lifted, a burden I had not even realized I was carrying. I had been anchored to a place I shouldn't have been. Now, obedience had set me free to go where I was meant to be.

Within days, my husband and I found ourselves at an awesome church, a church that has drawn us closer together as a couple and has opened doors for each of us to use the gifts God has given us to share. Walking in His will is a lesson on the importance of following His promptings, even when our flesh tries so hard to rebuke them. He has mapped out each of our lives from the beginning. His direction will *always* lead to the high road, where what is best for us will *always* be found.

You Were There

As I reread my life's story,
Turning back the pages of the years,
I see You by my side
Through all my happiness, through all my tears.

When I was a little child,
I looked to Heaven's Light
To protect me from the shadows
Of the terrifying nights.

And You Were there.

Becoming a young girl,
Striving to stifle emotional pain,
I looked to You for comfort,
Searching for any shreds of happiness that I could gain.

And You Were there.

Teetering on the brink of teenage years,
During the ups and downs of days,
I came to You for guidance
To lead me on my way.

And You Were there.

A high school and college student
In classes, struggling to do my best,
I asked You for comprehension
As I was challenged with each test.

And You Were there.

A woman on my wedding day
At the age of twenty-one,
I asked You to be with us
During the married years to come.

And You Were there.

In the moments when the doctor said, "You're pregnant!"
With our daughter, with our son,
I prayed for their safe arrival here
As we waited for each miracle to come.

And You Were there.

On the day I heard the words, "Daddy's gone!"
Through my mother's voice choked with tears,
In grief I grasped for You to Give me strength
For assurance that You Were Near.

And You Were there.

In the birth of every grandchild,
Could there be any joy to compare?
I asked that Your Love Surround them
And that You forever Keep them in Your Care.

And You Were there.

Time ticking away the moments
Toward my mother's drawing of her last breath,
My heart sobbed that You Carry her on Angel's wings
To her blessed Eternal rest.

And You Were there.

Storm-tossed times of torment
As I strived to do Your Will,
My soul screamed, "Please don't leave me!"
As all became so still.

Yet, You Were there.

Is it any wonder, then,
That when I think of You
I pause in sheer amazement
At the magnitude of Mercy in all You Do?

For You Are The Reason I live;
You Gave me my first breath.
You Knew me before my conception;
You Will be with me at the moment of my death.

You have always Walked beside me,
My Faithful Father, my Friend.
You have forever been there with me;
Your Unconditional Love You forever extend.

And so, Dear Jesus, As I've thought of my life's journey
And of all we have been through,
My heart sings out its Praises
In this poem, just *for You*.

Joshua 1:5

November 2010

Note on "You Were There"

I was questioning whether to include both the poems "Remembering" and "You Were There" in this book. At first glance, they seem to be very similar; they both relate very specifically to my life. Yet, I pray as you read each of them that the Lord will speak into *your* life. You will be able to identify with the words, just as I did when I "put them to paper." The little child, the young girl, the teenage years, the school years, the wedding day, the birth of children, the death of parents, stepping stones along the journey of life—whether man or woman, there will be parts of this poem that resonate within *your* spirit. As the memory goes back over the days of your own life, you will realize He Was there—and *is* there—for you, too.

The Disciple

My Jesus,

In the hours of deepest darkness,
In the middle of the night,
My spirit looks for answers
As it strives to see Your Light.

I wonder how You can love me
When all I tend to do
Is steep myself in selfishness,
Forgetting, ignoring You.

I pretend within myself
That I'm doing all I can,
But I can't pretend to You,
For You Know who I am.

You See me walking in delusion,
Wallowing in my weaknesses from day to day,
As You Wait, forever patiently,
For me to glance Your way.

Oh, I know You're there, My Jesus,
My forever Faithful Friend
I know Your Love for me is unconditional
And that it will never have an end.

I feel so unworthy
Of all You Have Done for me,
And though I keep on falling short,
It seems You Do not See.

Therein lies the miracle,
Though You Know me inside out.
Have You ever ceased to Love me?
Of this I have no doubt.

I just want to be Your disciple,
To do all that I can
To reach out unto others,
To be Your Feet and Hands.

My spirit is so willing to follow,
Yet my flesh continually lags behind.
Then I hear Your Gentle Whisper:
"Child, Remember that you are *Mine.*

"Do not look to your flesh for strength
To overcome what you cannot.
Place all your burdens in My Hands,
For there you will find the Peace you have sought.

"Do not feel alone in your struggles;
They are nothing new to Me.
I Have Watched the battle of flesh through the ages,
And Until the end The battle will be.

"Those I Chose to walk with Me
When I was upon this earth,
They, too, had their doubts and demons;
They, too, struggled with their worth.

"None of them was perfect;
I Knew that from the start.
The beauty that I Saw in them
Was found within their hearts.

"Though their spirits were forever willing,
Their flesh was so oftentimes weak.
What kept them upon My Path
Was that they never stopped being willing to *seek.*

"And this is true for each who has loved Me,
From My first disciple to those of today.
This is true of *you,* My Child,
As you journey on your way.

"I have Called you as My disciple,
As I Have Called each and every one,
Yet it Saddens Me to See
How few have actually come.

"This world of humanity's turmoil
Is filled with pain and strife.
When you act as My disciple,
You can make a change in someone's life.

"Not only someone, but many
Can come to know Who I Am.
They will see Me through your eyes;
They will feel My Presence through your outreached hands.

"Then, When their time on earth is done,
When they arrive at Heaven's Shore,
They will testify of how they found Me,
Of when they had come to be lost no more.

"They will tell of a glorious day
When they had stopped living merely to survive,
When they had met one of My disciples
Who had shown them I Am truly *alive*.

"When they had seen My Love as *living*,
Not merely read about it in The Pages of The Book,
When they had come to *truly* know Me
Through the time with them you took,

"Yes, it will have been *you*, My Precious Child,
Who helped Me save the lost
When you were willing to follow My Call
And do all that it might cost.

"To look beyond your weaknesses
To find your strength in Me,
To reach out unto others
So that My Image they might see.

"My Heart will be filled with Joy
When we meet at Heaven's Door.
As I Say, 'Well done, My good and faithful servant,'
You could have done no more."

Philippians 4:13

November 2010

Note on "The Disciple"

So many times we question, how can I make any difference? I'm just one person in an entire world. Anything I might try to do seems so insignificant. Then we think about our weaknesses, how we so oftentimes fall short and wonder how we can be an example in someone else's life when our own is in such a mess. Yet, when we truly become disciples of Jesus, *insignificant* becomes an outdated word, and our falling short doesn't apply anymore because now we draw all our strength from Him. When we begin placing *Him* first and are reaching out to others in *His* name, miracles begin to happen in our lives as well as in the lives of those we touch for Him. We become world-changers, and the world will be left a better place because we accepted His call to step out as one of His own.

Father, We seek Your Face and mercy
As these days of turmoil abound.
We ask You for Your Grace
In a covering of Peace profound.

The enemy relentlessly batters
At the door of every saint,
Gnawing at the seeds of faith,
Ceaselessly attacking so all grow faint.

Family members trapped by deceit
In the web of the world's lies,
Where once they followed in Your Steps
There is now darkness before their eyes.

Parents crying in the night
As they mourn their sons and daughters,
Relationships ripped to shreds
Between mothers, between fathers.

Bodies felled in illness,
Bringing the focus to the flesh.
The devil's derisive laughter
As trust endures its hardest test.

In the natural, as we are overwhelmed
With loss, destruction, and despair,
We call upon Your Name;
We need to know that You are there.

I pause now in this writing
Of these words cried from my heart.
I wait upon my Jesus,
And the following message He imparts:

"My child,

"As the time of the enemy grows short,
He is doing all he can
To cripple all My followers
To conclude his demonic plan.

"As the shroud of darkness hovers
Over so many homes and hearts,
Evil slithers as a snake,
Poisoning goodness in every part.

"Now I say, fear not, My beloved children,
For you never stand alone.
I have brought you to My Light;
I have called you as My Own.

"It is in the strongest opposition
That my power will be Revealed
Signs and Wonders will unfold;
As before My Throne you kneel.

"Do not contemplate the negatives
Of the circumstances you may see.
Lift your eyes to Heaven;
Focus them on Me.

"My Beloved Children, *press on in prayer*;
Hold the banner high.
The demonic will be defeated
As the fire of Truth consumes the lies.

"Guard your words with watchfulness;
Speak only those of faith.
Close the door to the demonic;
Open Heaven's Gate.

"My Beloved Children, I Am not there,
I Am *here*, Closer than the air you breathe.
I Am The Alpha and The Omega;
I Am The Answer to all your needs.

"Do not be discouraged;
Do not be dismayed.
The victory is won;
The price has all been paid.

"Good Friday, A time of darkness,
When no glimmer of hope was to be found.
In its circumstances, there appeared no triumph,
Only a destination of man's life into the ground.

"But *remember*, My Dear Children,
The outcome of that day.
Remember the sky of an Easter morning;
Remember the brilliance of Heaven's rays.

"The proof of the Promise fulfilled,
The victory over Satan's scheme,
This is the picture you are to hold in your hearts
As the battle becomes extreme.

"I Am the Alpha and the Omega;
I Am the Lamb Who was slain.
I Am your Redeemer;
The victory has already been gained.

"I Am the Answer for all creation;
I Am the Answer for all doubts.
I Am the Answer that shines deep within you,
While you only see darkness without.

"Focus on the manifestation of blessings
That from the ashes have come.
It is then you will see My Hand moving
In the miracles that have so clearly been done.

Revelation 21:6–7

January 2011

Note on "I AM ..."

The cord of the love of the great I AM flows throughout this poem, connecting heaven with earth. While we are so continually battered by this world's tribulations, we have His Promise. He was, He is, and He will *always remain;* all else pales in comparison. There is *no* battle that we may *ever* face that compares with the *incomparable* and *unconditional* love that He has for *each* of us. He has proven it through His death, He has proven it through His resurrection, and *He* continues to prove it through the blessings He pours into our lives. The great I Am, He alone is able to turn ashes into miracles with just one touch upon a life. The battle *has* been won; He holds the victory within His hands.

Praise Him, Praise Him,
Praise Him above all.
Praise Him, Praise Him
In all things great and small.

Praise Him in the night;
Praise Him in the day.
Praise Him for Who He Is;
Praise Him as The Way.

Praise Jesus as The Light;
Praise Jesus as The King.
Praise Jesus as The Savior;
Let His Praises *ring*!

Prepare the Path of Praise,
For The Lord is to arrive.
Prepare The Path of Praise
As you look upon the skies.

Hosannah in the Highest,
The host of Heaven sings.
Heaven is rejoicing;
Prepare the way for The King!

See the bright star shining in the east
Before the morning light.
See the picture of Heaven's Promise
That will soon dissolve the night.

Praise Him, Praise Him,
Praise Him more than ever before.
Praise Him, Praise Him,
Now and forevermore.

REVELATION 22:16

January 2011

Note on "Prepare the Path of Praise"

As I finished typing the last word of "Prepare the Path of Praise," I was led to the book of Revelation, 22:16. There I saw the following words and heard them *resonate* within my spirit. In one indescribable moment, I *felt* the touch of Jesus, the King of the universe, upon my heart, upon the very *essence* of my being, and there are no words to convey the awesomeness of it.

"I, Jesus, have sent mine angel to testify unto you these things in the churches. I Am the root and the offspring of David, *and the bright and morning star.*"

He is The Star; He is The Promise. He is All-Consuming Love. He is our Reason for being, and He is Coming. Let us prepare our hearts; let us prepare The Path of Praise.

I love You, Jesus, *to Thee be all the honor, all the glory, and all the praise forever.*

The Plea for the Family

These lines come with intensity,
With *urgency* and need.
These lines are meant for *all* to hear;
They are The Holy Spirit's heartfelt plea.

"Take your eyes off of this world's darkness,
Carried in the shadows by the prince of evil.
See the good that I have Created
Awaken to all that he has come to steal.

"Do not be deceived
By the lure of Satan's lies.
His time is growing short
As his last attempts he tries.

"*Awake* to what is happening
In your home and in your hearts.
Awake and look around you,
For the battle has had its start.

"His ways are smooth as silk
As he destroys families one by one,
Coming against their unity
Blinding them of the destruction to come.

"This is the root of evil
In these last, these final days:
The destruction of the family tree,
Branches brittled and decayed.

"HEAR ME NOW:

"Gather your children around you,
Both the old as well as young.
Strengthen the foundation of love's beginning;
Heed not the devil's lying tongue.

"What I have Joined together
No man is to put asunder.
Satan has come to steal and destroy,
All marriage vows to plunder.

"Yet I Say:

"Do not be dismayed, My Child,
If you have been deceived within his scheme.
Make this moment your new beginning;
Awaken from his dark dream.

"Love one another as I have Loved you;
Love is the way to My Light.
Love Everlasting is all that I Am;
Seek Me to make *all* things right.

Acts 3:25

March 2011

Note on "The Plea for the Family"

This poem is specifically written to couples with children. When a family shatters, there are many more than two lives affected. The hearts of children are broken, those so close to the heart of Jesus. And I am convinced He speaks His plea through this poem. Protect them, love them, let them not be swept away on the sands of selfishness and deceit, a sinking foundation built upon Satan's lies. The family bond is meant to be an enduring and beautiful reflection of the love He has for us, a bond forever solidified in and through Him. All the families upon this earth are meant to be *blessed,* unified within His love.

Footsteps to The Cross

When life for you has become too hard,
When you think you can't go one more step,
Remember the footsteps to Calvary;
Think of what *each* footstep meant.

Each step was made with Love for *you*,
Upon tattered feet throbbing in piercing pain.
He carried His Love bent under a cross,
Wearing garments with blood-soaked stains.

In my spirit, I see the crowd gathered,
Pressing in on all sides as He passed by,
Some sobbing with grief uncontrollable,
Many more mocking, believing the lie.

As The Lamb went to His slaughter,
He uttered not a *single* word.
He could have cried out for deliverance;
His Father would surely have Heard.

Yet He persevered on that cruel road before Him,
To the hill where He was to be slain.
Each step He Made was Selfless.
For Him, there was *nothing* to be gained.

As Golgotha drew nearer,
As He could walk no more,
They dragged Him to the final place
As His followers begging for mercy implored.

But there was to be no mercy on that day
At the place the footsteps stopped.
There was only a shredded body upon a cross
Marking the ending place of the battle fought.

His Love endured until the end;
With His last breath, He thought of *you*, of *me*.
Every drop of His Blood had been shed
So that in Eternity with Him we could be.

The price had been paid by The Lamb Who was slain;
Our salvation He had secured.
Our peace, joy, and freedom were purchased that day
Through the unimaginable brutality Jesus endured.

When we think we walk alone
And that no one understands,
He Whispers, "*Remember* that day on Calvary;
Remember all it cost to defeat Satan's plan.

"When your footsteps become weary,
When you think that no one cares,
Call upon My Name,
For in your burdens I *Long* to share.

"I Cared enough to die for *you*,
To Give *all* I Could Give.
I did it all to show My Love
So *you* could fully live.

John 17:1–2

January 2011

Background of "Footsteps to The Cross"

A woman in our church had been very ill and was hospitalized for several weeks. When she was able to come back to church, she shared with the congregation a vision she had while she was in the hospital. She had seen Jesus taking the steps that led Him to the cross, His footsteps going to the Cross. I had just written this poem; no one had yet heard it. There was no doubt in my mind that the Lord had me write it *for her*. The moment I gave her the poem was a blessing beyond compare for me, as I contemplated the meaning between her vision and the confirmation through the poem. I believe Jesus was telling her, "I know you are suffering; I too suffered. I walked alone, but you will never be alone in your trials. I am with you through *every* step," just as He is with each of us.

Judie's Song

Dear Jesus, It's happened once again.
I have been blessed beyond compare.
You have crossed my path with yet another,
Another who is truly of You aware.

She walks within Your Footsteps;
She listens to Your Voice.
She places her self aside
As she makes Your Desire her only choice.

From the day that she was saved,
She has left her life behind.
She has offered it all to You, Lord,
Family, friends, and time.

How many have come to know *You*
Through the vessel that *she* has been?
How many have turned their lives to You
And renounced the way of sin?

She is Your faithful follower,
Of this there is no doubt.
Your Love she holds within her heart
Manifests so brilliantly Your Light without.

And so it is no wonder, Lord,
That You have Called her as Your Own,
Through all that she has done for You,
Through all the seeds that she has sown.

Within Your Heavenly Realm,
As the host of Heaven sings,
I can hear Your Proclamation:
"To her A special gift I Will Bring.

"I Will Give to her a stream of melodies
To sing within My Word.
Many will be touched by this;
My Voice will be Clearly Heard.

"As she teaches My little children,
As she ministers to all,
My Blessings will flow abundantly,
For she has been the answer to My Call.

"I Will strengthen her and bless her;
I Will Raise her above the storms.
I Will Carry her over mountains;
I Will *never* Leave her forsaken nor forlorn.

"She is My Precious Child;
She has loved Me for so long.
I Treasure her as My vessel;
I AM in Judie's song."

Romans 4:20

February 2011

Background of "Judie's Song"

I have a precious friend named Judie. She is one of the most faith-filled people I have ever met. As she endures trials, words of faith flow through her speech. One of the many gifts the Lord has instilled within her is to put words of Scripture into song. At the time of my writing this, she had been bedridden for several weeks with an illness. Following is the description of how far God reached to touch her heart and fill it with continued encouragement. I know He is using this as an example for *each* of us, to remind us that He is closer to us and cares more for us than we could ever imagine. (I present the following just as it was written on that weekend.)

This weekend, the Lord has focused my spirit on the gift of song within Scripture that He has given to Judie. On Saturday afternoon, I was asking Him to lead me to some words of encouragement for her, and I came across a little book I hadn't seen in years entitled *Little Taps on the Shoulder from God*. In it, I found the following Scripture:

"God is the One Who saves me:
I will trust Him and not be afraid.
The Lord, the Lord gives me strength
And makes me sing!" (Isaiah 12:2).

My spirit leapt, as I *knew* this was meant for her. Later that night, we were watching television. At the beginning of this particular program, they always read a Scripture promise for the day. As they read the following words, *again* my Spirit leapt as the Lord confirmed within me that *this* too was for Judie:

"The Lord is my strength and my shield:
My heart trusted in Him, and I am helped:
Therefore, my heart greatly rejoiceth:
And with my song will I praise Him" (Psalm 28:7).

Then came Sunday morning. When I awoke, I began asking the Lord, "What can I bring to Judie? Another plant? Dinner? Lord, I need something that will really touch her spirit, and I'm feeling so inadequate right now in my attempts to offer encouragement." And so the Lord was about to teach me a lesson, to bring me to the realization that I *was* inadequate, but that *He is not.* He was about to fill in that space where I had nothing to give. For, before very few minutes had passed, a poem had started. The words poured out into verses surrounding the beautiful gift He has given Judie in her Scripture-filled songs.a very special treasure shared between a very godly woman and her Father .I was blessed beyond measure to pen the words of this poem that so lovingly flow from His heart to hers.

Today I stop to realize
How *blessed* I have come to be
Through The Touch of God upon my life,
Through His Opening my eyes to see.

As I turn the pages back
To the beginning of the story,
Each encounter becomes a stepping stone
To the manifestation of today's Glory.

I see His Revelation
Reflected in the mirror of my soul.
He Has Destroyed each attempt of the enemy
To steal what He Has Made whole.

The remembrances are written so clearly,
I "see" them line by line.
The messages flow with a Love so *intense*,
Undimmed by the passage of time.

"My child, I Have Been with you
Since the day you came to be.
Through *all* that you have been through,
You have walked each day with Me.

"You have not always known My Presence;
There were times you thought I Had Gone
As you stumbled through those endless nights
When the torment seemed so long.

"My Light has ALWAYS been here,
But your closed "eyes" could not see.
In your fear and doubt, you faltered;
You just lost sight of Me.

"I Have Walked with you through *each* sorrow
From the time that you were small.
When you thought you had no Father,
I was there to hear your call.

"I Gave you Peace within
When there was none to see without.
You *felt* My Hand upon you;
I Left you with no doubt.

"When you saw yourself as less than others,
When you struggled to make things right,
I *never* Left your side;
You never left My Sight.

"Through the myriad of emotional battles
When you thought you had been wronged,
I touched the sorrow in your heart;
I Replaced it with a song.

"That moment you came to place Me first
I never will forget,
The moment you *fully* recognized Me
As heart to Heart we met.

"In that moment, Were the trials over?
No, With *more* intensity they had begun.
Darkness and doubt swirled around you,
But *now* you kept your eyes upon The Son.

"When others questioned your actions,
I Gave you the strength to stand.
Now you knew you could not falter
If you were to remain within My Plan.

"I Brought you through the trials,
Poured out in a torrent of your tears,
As the storm broke forth in rainbows,
As My Voice Rang Out *so clear.*

"When there were those who talked against you
For what you had done for Me,
I *closed* their mouths of judgment,
Bringing others to plainly see.

"You asked Me for My Guidance,
For wisdom to discern,
To know My Will within your life,
To seek Me at every turn.

"And so today you see the fruit
Of what your Faith has done.
Drawing others to My Heart,
Their Salvation to be won."

My response flows through my spirit:

Dear Father,

My gratefulness is *endless*
On this day above all days,
As my husband seeks Your Face,
As he strives to know your ways.

For Your Plan from the beginning
Was *never* just for me;
You Seek the love of *each* of us,
Of *all* my family.

So today Your Touch is Gentle
Upon my husband's heart;
Today a prayer is answered
That so long ago had its start.

Time to You means nothing;
The past is washed away.
Your Love for us is in *this moment,*
In the miracle of today.

Lamentations 3:22–23

May 2011

Note on "Today"

The poem "Today" is a testimony to God's forever-faithfulness. My prayer is that, as you read, you will feel the verses flow through your spirit and unfold within the context of your own life. May you be washed in the river of His love, His mercy, and His compassion as they stream through the lines. If you are experiencing struggles and holding on to long-held promises, may these words from the throne assure you that faith is *never* in vain and that the harvest *will* come, that what you may have only hoped for yesterday is destined to become a reality in your soon-to-be today.

The Answer to All Questions

A question has been knocking
At the entrance of my heart.
The sound is soft and gentle;
I'm not sure when it had its start.

The question asks, "I wonder?"
I wonder where I would be
If You had given up Calling for me?
If You had not Opened my eyes to see?

Where would I be at this time in my life,
Walking in this world of today?
Would I be drowning in desperation in humanity's sea,
Slowly sinking in my self-made ways?

Would I be shrouded in negatives, stumbling in the dark,
Trapped in a cave with air running out?
Would I scream out in my terror, only to find
That there was no one to hear my shouts?

Would I see other lives as empty as mine
Continually running yet knowing not where?
Would I feel crushed in the crowd of millions of people,
Yet starving for just one person to care?

Where would I be if I looked at the sky
And did not see the Touch of Your Hand?
Where would I be had I not stopped to seek,
To find You in all creation's plan?

Where would I be had I not found Your Love,
As Real as the stars in the sky?
Where would I be had Satan triumphed
In deluding me to believe all his lies?

Where would I be as the days swiftly flew
To the moment I took my last breath,
To the end of my time, when my eyes would be closed
In the finality of this world's death?

Who would I be, and where would I go?
These are questions I don't have to ask,
For Jesus, You are My Shepherd, The Guide of my life,
From its first day until its last.

You are The Answer to every question;
You are The Completion to every rhyme.
You are The Greatest Song that will ever be sung;
You are The Creator of all time.

You are The Maker of my destiny;
You are The Author of my life's story.
Your Heavenly home is my destination,
And to Thee, Lord, I give all the glory.

As I complete this last line,
As I lay down my pen,
I believe that this poem
Has come to an end.

"Not So," Jesus Whispers,
As He Says, "There is more.
You must continue this message
To express The Love I Implore.

"Where will *he* be if *you* do not reach out
To draw him to My Light?
Where will *she* be if *you* do not tell her of Me?
Will she be forever blinded by this world's night?

"You see, My Child, You are Precious to Me,
But I Am Calling to *each* one."
Yet without you reaching out to them,
They will *never* hear Me Say, 'Come.'

"*Come* unto Me, All you who are lost;
I Am The Answer you seek.
Lay down your burdens, your grief, and your guilt;
Come to Me and be made complete.

"For I Am Love Eternal,
A Love you cannot yet fully comprehend.
My Love for you was from the beginning;
My love for you will *never* have an end.

"Once you seek Me, you *will* find Me;
Your questions will melt away.
You will see Me as your Answer;
You will *know I* Am The Way."

John 14:6
Luke 19:10

May 2011

Note on "The Answer to All Questions"

I believe the Lord gave me this poem to paint a picture of His longing to embrace each of us within His love. I pour out my expression of thanksgiving that I know Him because I realize that I would be totally lost without Him. But, as He gently reminds me, what of those who *don't* know, who may *never* know unless I reach out to them in His name? Each of these is just as precious as I am to Him. Thank You for this reminder, Lord. It's not all about *me*. Rather, it's all about *us*, for *each* of us is Your heart's desire, and each of us is meant to reach out to others, forming a never-ending circle of Your Love.

The Battle is His

Dear Jesus, I seek Your Love and Guidance
Each moment of the day.
I pray they burn within me
As they shine to light my way.

When my eyes open to morning
From the visions of the night,
I offer each day to you;
I strive to do what's right.

But today the enemy is pounding
At the doorway of my soul;
His lying tongue pleads entrance
To steal all of gold.

As he sees the lock is more secure
Than ever in times past,
A torrent of torment begins to gush forth,
As with hissing whispers he starts to lash,

"You cannot stand in triumph;
I know where you have been.
I was with you every step you walked
As you fell deeper into sin.

"To think that you can overcome
What you have battled for so long—
Don't you see it is impossible?
It is so much easier to come along.

"Come along the road that is smooth and wide,
Where so many others walk.
There are no limits here;
There are no boundaries or locks.

"Where you live your life for you;
That's all that matters in the end.
The only worth you'll ever have
Is what in *this* world you can spend."

As he sees this deceit will no longer work
To pull me from my path,
He shrieks out for more demons
Filled with hatred, filled with wrath.

Demons of discouragement,
Depression, and despair
Begin their vile venom
As they come from everywhere.

I try to drown out their sickening sounds
Before they find "cracks" within my mind,
Any opening to seep their deadly poison in,
Any entrance they can find.

Though I thought myself to be so strong,
I can feel myself becoming weak.
The rantings are relentless
As the fiendish force of evil speaks.

The joy that I once had
Begins to slip away.
Shattering peacefulness breaks around me
As I sink in my dismay.

As I am drawn deeper into darkness,
As I can fight no more,
The light within my spirit is flickering;
Only One Word can I implore:

JESUS! I cry out
In my misery and fear.
I cannot see His Presence;
I do not know if He Hears.

But wait!

Deep within my spirit,
Do I hear the rustle of Angels' wings?
I feel the shift within my soul
As the Call to Battle rings!

For The Lord Has Called His Warriors
To fight The Holy Fight.
My strength becomes renewed
As I lean upon their might.

Michael and Gabriel stand in shining armor,
Their swords uplifted toward The Son,
With words of affirmation:
"The battle has been won!"

They speak in tones of *thunder*;
From Heaven's Realm they come.
*"Satan, depart now from this Child of God;
This soul you have not won!*

"This one lives for The Lord above,
Covered by The Blood of the Lamb.
This one dwells in Heaven's Light,
In the Heart of the Great I Am.

"This one has named Jesus as her Savior,
The Name above all names.
Your temptations are *all* futile;
Go back from where you came."

Time stands still within this space
As I sense the Love and Mercy of my God's Grace.
All I see are My Savior's Eyes
As Satan and his demons sink into their pool of lies.

2 Chronicles 20:15
1 Samuel 17:47

May 2011

Note on "The Battle is His"

This poem speaks of the never-ending battle that rages daily for the victory over our souls. Satan's favorite place of battle is our mind, where he can bombard us with all types of doubt, discouragement, and despair. And so many times we allow him to, making little effort to "take up our shield," many times forgetting we even have one until it is almost too late. His hope is that if he can sink us down deep enough in the water of his murky lies, we won't have enough strength to ever get back to the surface, to grip the life preserver of our faith. But the Lord knew what perilous times we would have to pass through while living in this world, and so He provided us with a weapon that will *never* fail, is easily accessible, and is carried within us. In times of peril, we just have to call upon His name—Jesus, the Name above all others, our Shield, our Deliverer, our Conqueror.

"I Am The Good Shepherd,
The Way, The Truth, The Light.
I Am here to guide you
Through each moment of your life.

"Then, When this earthly journey
Has come to its determined end,
I Will Continue to Guide you
Into the Eternity together we will spend.

"The one you mourn for here today
Now rests within My Arms.
For them, there is no longer suffering or grief;
They can experience *no more* harm.

"Their worldly journey is finished
As the sunset ends a day;
They have *seen* the sunrise of heaven's morning
As they shed their flesh of clay.

"But for you whose tears are falling
Within your broken hearts,
All you can see is a life ended
When it was much too soon to part.

"I Am The Good Shepherd;
My sheep I do not leave.
I Am with you through all time;
I Am with you as you grieve.

"The hour is to come
When you will see each loved one once again.
Then I Will Be there to rejoice with you
As your sorrow comes to its *final* end.

"I Will Dry each tear you have cried;
All pain of separation will be gone.
I Will Turn your mourning into dancing;
I Will Replace it with a song.

"I Am The Good Shepherd;
All of my Promises are true.
My Love for you is *endless*;
I will make *all* things new.

"The destiny of death is not into darkness;
Rather, it is the transition into the light.
It is the beginning of eternity;
It is the end of *all* terror and fright

"It is awakening to Eternal morning
Inside The Heavenly Gates;
It is beauty *beyond* human description.
It is The Promise for which *you* wait.

"Death has been defeated
Through the Sacrifice I made.
Look within My Word;
You will see the Price I paid.

Psalm 23

June 2011

Note on "Heaven's Sunrise"

How the Lord loves each of us! His hand is upon *every* moment of our lives. He longs for us to fully realize how much He loves us, to fully know that *everything* we experience, He experiences: the joy, the victories, the pain, the sorrow. He has touched my heart with the intensity of how He grieves with us when a loved one has gone on. His heart breaks with ours as we experience empty spaces that were once filled. He grieves for us because we do not yet comprehend; we do not yet have the capability to fully understand what is to come. It is only when we make our own transition into eternity with Him that He will be able to show us what He has so longed for us to know, how He has so longed to wipe each tear we have cried.

The poem "Heaven's Sunrise" is the intense expression of the sorrow He experiences with us while we are still in the flesh and the tremendous joy He anticipates sharing with us as we join our loved ones in eternity. He emphasized in my spirit how important it is that the twenty-third psalm be read with this poem. To reiterate the message, *He is The Good Shepherd; He has never led us astray, and He never will.*

In This Place

My Dear child,

I Have Brought you to this moment,
Time set aside to seek My Face.
You are My vessel to be filled with Love and Mercy;
You are a receptacle of My Out-Pouring Grace.

May you gather all your thoughts today,
Placing each within My Heart.
May we live one inside Another
Until We cannot be told apart.

May you be led to My Holy Spirit;
May you be *filled* with The Love I Came to Show.
May My Flame that Lights your path
Set another's heart aglow.

May you hear My Whisper within the wind
As it moves throughout the trees;
May you sense My Voice Gently Calling
As you pray upon your knees.

May you know the depths of My Love for *you*
In a way you have *never* known before.
May you have steadfast assurance
That no one could *ever* love you more.

May you find Me in The Silence;
May you see Me in another's face.
May you know without a doubt
Why I Have Brought you to this place.

To seek Me and to find Me,
To lay your burdens down,
To find that you are *never* alone,
To *rest* in My Peace Profound.

As you live within each moment
In the time of this Retreat,
May your cup be filled with overflowing Joy
As in this place We meet.

Matthew 7:8

July 2011

Background of "In This Place"

As part of last year's women's retreat, instead of the women receiving letters from different people, it was suggested that each receive a copy of a poem. We discussed this at the first meeting of the retreat committee on Thursday, June 30. I had no doubt that the Lord would honor our request for this poem; I just had no idea when it might be given. As with every poem in the past, it came within His timing at 5:30 a.m. on Monday, July 4, Independence Day, a day that is built around the concept of *freedom*. Pondering this, I knew there was significance in the message being written on *this* day, for *this* retreat, in *this* season of *each* woman's life. The Lord wants us to know that as we seek Him, we will find Him and experience a *freedom* we have yet to know as we live, as we move, as we have our being in Him.

As we "retreat" to rest in Him, we will become *free* from bondages, hindrances, deceptions, and distractions of the enemy; *free* to be who we truly are in Him; *free* from the delusion that we have to meet someone else's expectations to find our own self-worth. Our worth comes not through the eyes of others but through *His eyes*. In *His eyes,* we are and always have been *all* we *ever* need to be—*precious, worthy, and loved beyond human comprehension.* At this retreat, we experienced the "Independence Day" He has always longed for us to have.

Renewal

My Child,

As Our time together here comes to an end,
There is nothing to compare
With our hearts drawn ever closer
In this time that we have shared.

As you walk back within the world,
Your heart's flame will be burning brighter.
Shadows will begin to fade away;
Your burdens will be so much lighter.

Strengthened through My Word,
Having taken time to seek My Face,
You are *now* prepared for battle,
Ready to claim the victory through My Grace.

The enemy is quaking;
His lies will no longer stand.
During your time here, your Faith has been fortified;
You have clarified vision to see My Plan

Remember that I Walk with you
Through *every* moment of your way.
Your spirit has been renewed;
It is the dawn of a new day.

Ephesians 2:8

September 2011

Background of "Renewal"

When the first poem was written for the beginning of the retreat, I sensed in my spirit that there would also be another poem given for the end. The above was written on 8/26/11, late in the evening. Within five minutes of writing the words *"The enemy is quaking"*, an earthquake actually occurred. Was this a coincidence, or rather a confirmation by The One Who Holds the universe in His Hands?

Rise Up!

I Am The Good Shepherd;
I Came to save the lost.
The sacrifice was brutal;
See how much it cost.

The world is full of "wolves,"
Lurking and leering, waiting to devour
My sheep who wander aimlessly,
Who have no strength, no power.

Saints, do not grow weary in prayer!

Prayer is voicing My Promise
That I Will be with you until the end.
Prayer is My firm affirmation
That in *this* world you will see My Hand Extend.

Prayer calls forth My legion of Angels
To surround you with their might.
Prayer is the two-edged sword of the battle
Prevailing over the demonic throughout day and night.

My Holy Spirit Hovers
In Flames of Fire to Fall.
Keep your heart from compromise;
I Am Waiting for your call.

Read My Word; walk in My Word.
Commit it to your heart.
Strengthen the bond I have with you;
Continually strive to do *your* part.

You will rise up on wings as eagles
As you place your trust in Me.
Victory will follow victory
As My Might and Power you will *clearly* see.

Show Love for your fellow man
As you strive to fully see
For I Am The Living Light of Love,
Unconditional Love I Am *forever* to be.

Rise up in the power of prayer;
Rise up with no compromise.
Rise up in the Love I have shown;
Rise up and destroy Satan's lies.

Rise up, My faithful followers;
Hypocrisy will no longer stand.
The Dawn of a New Day approaches,
The fulfillment of Heaven's Plan.

Hebrews 11:32–34

August 2011

Note on "Rise Up!"

The message of "Rise Up!" rings out clearly. The Lord is calling us to a heightened state of spiritual awareness. We can no longer afford to keep our eyes closed to what is happening around us; we can no longer sit idly by, hoping things will get better. It is in this state that we become easy prey for the enemy of our souls. The time is *now* to take up the weapon of *prayer,* to *rise up,* standing *firmly* on the foundation of the Word. The time has come when a *clear* line will be drawn between those who are true believers and those who are not. Our Shepherd waits for us to follow, bringing as many as possible into His flock, before "now" becomes "too late."

Father, Do You Hear Me?

So many different voices,
Yet each feeling so alone.
Engulfed in cries, in sobbing,
Hearts slowly turning into stone.

So many voices imploring,
So many broken apart.
Each wanting so desperately to change things,
Yet not knowing where to start.

Father, Where I once held hope and promise
Now all I have are empty hands.
Where I once saw my reflection,
Now I don't know who I am.

Father, Where once there was a couple,
I now find myself alone.
I live here in an empty house
That once was called a home.

Father, Ferocious fear stings within my soul,
As the chill of winter on bare skin,
Continually hammering in my meandering mind,
Pacing to and fro, lurking, waiting to rush in.

Father, I have lost a child;
They were not meant to go on before me.
How could this ever have happened?
How could this ever be?

Father, My life is *filled* with twists and turns;
So many addictions hold me in their tight fists.
Though I claw my way up from the deep, dark pit,
I so often find myself beginning to slip.

Father, Someone I shared my life with
Chose to take their own.
How could I not have seen the signs?
How could I not have known?

Father, I *cannot* stand this continuous pain
To torture me for one more day.
My life has no more substance
As upon this bed I lay.

Father, My life is now so broken,
Scattered in pieces across my soul.
Can it ever again be "fixed?"
Will I ever again feel whole?

Father, My child is on a downward spiral,
Spinning more out of control with each day.
I thought I had been a good parent;
I thought I had shown them the right way.

Father, Forgive, Forgive, Forgive;
I am drowning in the bottom of this dark sea.
It is not that I am unable to forgive others,
It is that I can see no forgiveness for me.

Father, The specter of depression
Is choking me with its cloak.
I can see no more of daylight
As it clutches at my throat.

Father, Father, Father!
Voices wailing in despair,
"Father, Do you hear me?
Or are You even there?"

Or are You even there? … or are You even there? …
The echo continues on and on.
Resounding in the emptiness,
The emptiness where evil shows itself so strong.

Yet, In the stillness of this sadness,
In the deepness of this dark,
Someone is intently Listening
To the beating of *each* heart.

Though no words may ever be spoken,
He Knows *all* that is held within.
He Knows *each* path of torment;
He Knows where *each* life has been.

His Eyes are Pools of Compassion,
With a depth that has no end.
He Hears the moaning of all His Creation
As He Longs for each heart to mend.

Within this Stillness, within this Silence, He Softly begins to Speak:

"Yes, My child, I have heard your desperate cries
Within the shadows of this place.
I Have been Waiting here for you
With an abundance of My Grace.

"I Am your Loving Father,
Closer than the air you breathe.
I bring you strength and comfort
In your each and every need.

"I Am here to carry your burdens;
My Light is here to show
That my love for you is endless,
More *immense* than you will ever know.

"I will still your cries and quiet your fears;
Come, rest here in My Arms.
When you trust in Me with all your heart,
The enemy can do you *no more* harm.

"I will soften the hardness of the heart
That he so fiercely tried to bring;
Your fears will be forever washed away
As to my cross you cling.

"Deception lies in darkness,
But I Am drawing you to My Light.
The devil is defeated;
This is the finish of your thought-to-be endless night.

"I Am bringing you a Peace
That you have never known before.
I Am bringing you the assurance
That no one could *ever* Love you more.

"Yes, My Child, I have heard;
I never *once* left you alone.
Now take My Hand as we carry on;
I Am leading you safely home."

Romans 8:37

September 2011

Background of "Father, Do You Hear Me?"

The writing of "Father, Do You Hear Me?" differs from almost all the other poems written to date. Where most of the others were written in minutes, this one was written over the course of eight days. I know one of the most significant aspects of this poem is the timing of *when* it was written; the first verse came on Monday, Sept. 19, 2011, the same day I was diagnosed with pneumonia, and the last verse came eight days later on the day I went back to resuming my "normal" life, after having been confined by the illness.

The timing of the message proclaimed throughout this poem is *clear*: our God is not confined within *any circumstances*. What the enemy had intended to use to bring weakness, the Lord has transformed into one more opportunity to manifest His love that *never fails*, His mercy for *all* who cry out to Him, His assurance that *He has not left us and that He never will. Jesus is the shield* against *all* that is devised to kill, steal, weaken, and destroy our faith, Whether it be an illness or one of the other circumstances voiced in the poem or one of the millions of other situations through which humanity suffers, *no circumstance can ever overcome His unconditional love for us. He hears us.* He is waiting patiently *for us to hear Him, to take His hand, and to fear no more.*

Ministering Angels

Ministering angels are circling 'round,
Called by The Master to do His Will.
They have not come to rest in this earthly place
Because it is yet not quiet, not still.

Ministering angels Waiting outside
To enter the room of the sick,
Yet the space is too filled with the works of the flesh;
The atmosphere stifled and thick.

The Lord Looks on the scene with His Eyes Filled with Love,
Knowing the hurt and the pain.
His Voice Gently Whispers, "Won't you please step aside?
For only *then* can I Send Healing Rain.

"Your loved one calls out and you rush to her side
To provide help in any and every way;
In your striving to bring comfort, you find no rest for yourself,
And you cannot hear what I Would Say.

"Peace, My Child, be still and know
That I Am with you through it *all*.
I Know of your fears, and I Know of your need;
I have heard you when you have called.

"Release, Release, Release,
You must rest within My Plan.
You carry Me in your heart;
You know Me as the Great I Am.

"Your loved one is a precious gift
I have Given you for a time.
Her years on earth have been with you,
But she is and will forever be Mine.

"Rest in this assurance, My Child,
That when you are not at your mother's side,
She is *never* alone; you have *nothing* to fear.
My ministering angels abide.

My vigil is never-ending;
You may close your eyes in sleep.
My angels are attending
As the heavenly watch they keep.

2 Thessalonians 3:16
Psalm 91:11–12

December 2011

Background of "Ministering Angels"

The mother of a friend had a stroke and was in the hospital. Her daughter was exhausted physically and emotionally, as she had barely left her mother's side for days. When I walked into the hospital room, the first thing my friend asked was, "Leta, do you have a poem for me?" I told her yes, thinking I would choose from the ones that had already been written. I wasn't aware that the Lord had other plans. Two hours after arriving back home, I had a poem just for her. Once again, the words flowed from my spirit within minutes; "Ministering Angels" is the result.

A few days after giving my friend this poem, she called to tell me how overwhelmed with gratefulness she was in having received it. Reading the words had brought her to the point of release; she was now able to rest in the Lord's promise that her mother was being held in His loving care. She went on to say that her mother had awoken in the hospital that morning and said, "My room is full of angels!" All the suffocating concern that had been held in that place had been released to the Lord. Now, His angels had room to come in.

The devil's derisive laughter
Fills the chasm of the pit
That place of deepest darkness
Where no candle can be lit.

He hisses to his demons
As they shriek with hideous glee.
They are looking upon the earth,
Upon the picture that they see.

"Look at those 'believers,'" Satan snarls,
"Who have been following their so-called king.
They had no idea what their choice would cost them;
They had not a clue as to what I would bring!

"I have stuffed their days with desperation;
I have pierced their nights with pain.
I have eroded their emotions;
I have stripped them of all that they had gained!

"Their resolve is about to crumble;
They will soon be wallowing in the world's ways.
They will forget all about The Son of God;
They will come to serve *me* for the rest of their days!

"Then when their listless lives are over
And there's nothing left to say,
Their souls will slip into my inferno,
Where for eternity they will stay!"

His eyes of red flame with hideous hatred
As he converses with his fiends,
Relishing the plight of once faith-filled Christians
Succumbing to his slithering schemes.

Suddenly, In an instant, with no warning,
The portals of hell begin to quake.
Lightening crashes through the pitch-blackness;
A Voice enveloped in mighty thunder Reverberates:

"Satan, father of deceit!

"Have you forgotten My beloved Job,
Who endured all you would send?
Have you forgotten Who had the victory,
Who had triumphed in the end?

"My Word is *filled* with Promises;
My Children *know* them to be true.
I have told them of the trials
They are assured of passing through.

"They know they will pass through them;
They were never meant to stay.
They abide in My Love and Grace;
My Mercy enfolds them *every* day.

"No matter what may come,
Their righteousness *will* stand.
My sheep will *always* hear My Voice;
They know of Who I Am.

"My warring angels are with them,
Surrounding them on all sides.
The hedge is high around them
As My Light penetrates *all* your lies.

"They are washed in My Blood,
Redeemed by the Cross.
Their ransom is *complete;*
I have Paid *all* the cost.

"Death has been defeated;
There is no power in its sting.
Devil of deception,
There is *nothing* you can bring.

"They call upon their Jesus,
And they know that I Am *here*.
They have *no* doubts within them
That *all* their cries I Hear."

With the mention of *that* Name,
The Name Above them all
Satan and all his demons flee in terror
As deeper into the pit they fall.

Falling further and yet further,
They are still tortured by the ring
As the voices of all God's Children
Sing out in praises to their King.

Ephesians 6:16

December 2011

Background of "Endless Victory"

On Tuesday morning, December 6, I was suddenly overcome with sadness for so many people around me who had been enduring so many trials. I asked the Lord, "How long, Lord? These are *good* people, whose hearts have served you for so long. When will these trials be over for them?" Tears were running down my face when I heard clearly within my spirit, *"Remember Job."* Within five minutes, the words of this poem were flowing out. To Him be *all the glory* for yet one more manifestation of His endless love for us as He assures us that *the victory is forever ours, in Him.*

Believe

Father, I have waited here so long
For You to Hear my cry.
You have given me *no* answer;
It seems You have passed me by.

There was a time I had such faith;
I *clearly* heard Your Voice.
My life was filled with blessings;
You were my One and Only Choice.

I placed You first within my life;
Higher ... There was *no* other.
My joy was to read Your Holy Word,
To find all the Truths I could discover.

But that life now seems so long ago,
So far away, so lost.
I never imagined the pain to come;
I never imagined what sacrifice cost.

Now my trust in You is torn to bits;
My faith, It has faded away.
My heart is pierced with desperation;
There is no light left within my days.

The Father's Tears are falling
As His child slips away.
He longs that she would wait
To *hear* what He would Say.

"My daughter, I would *never* leave you;
I Created you with such care.
You are My shining jewel;
You have beauty beyond compare.

"I Know this time of waiting
Seems an eternity to you,
But *believe*, My Cherished Child,
For *all* My Promises are true.

"I will *never* leave you nor forsake you,
No matter *what* circumstances may be.
Seek Me from within,
For it is *there* that you will *see*.

"*Believe* that I Work *all* for good
In ways that you cannot yet see.
In the worst you can imagine.
You can *always* trust in Me.

"You feel your broken body
Is crippled beyond repair;
You feel that no one can comprehend,
That in understanding your pain, no one can share.

"You say you have no more strength,
That you can no longer stand.
Draw *all* your strength from Me;
I Am the Great I Am.

"Look to *Me*, My Child,
Remember where I was.
I hung upon a Cross;
I paid the cost for Love.

"When My Body was ripped in pieces,
When I could stand no more,
I, too, cried out in desperation;
I, too, My Father implored.

"'*Why have You fosaken Me?*'
I Asked within My final breaths.
My suffering seemed so senseless
To many who were witnessing My death.

"But within those 'seeds of sadness,'
Within the darkness of that day,
Dawn was just over the horizon,
The Light of Resurrection's Rays.

"So *Remember*, My dear child,
Appearances are *not* what they would seem.
You know Me as the Healer;
I have shown you in your dreams.

"Look within My Word;
Read of all the Healings.
For Me to do restoration,
You *must* keep on believing.

"The enemy is attempting
To draw you from My Word;
Read My Scriptures *daily*,
Loudly to be heard.

"Your faith will be renewed;
You will *know* I Am by your side.
I Am the Great I Am;
Forever I will abide."

1 Peter 2:21

December 2011

Background of "Believe"

This was written when I was told about a woman who was severely debilitated by a disease. Once a strong, faith-filled Christian, she had given up on God and His promises. She felt it had been too long (over two years)and that an answer would never come, healing would never come, and her suffering would never end. Though I had never met this woman, tears streamed down my face as I thought of her situation. This poem is the Lord's response to her, a call to remember the suffering *He* endured for us, a plea to remember that His promises *are* true and that joy *will* come in the morning. Whether you are His daughter or His son, He is Holding you within His heart.

The Time In-Between

Father, My life is upside down
For so many different reasons.
How long must I "hold on?"
How long will be this "season?"

In the past, I have seen Your Mighty Hand;
I know You to be Good, to be Great,
But in this time of tests and trials,
It is so *hard* to endure the wait.

It seems that each new day
Brings more burdens I have to bear.
Where once I felt whole and strong,
I now feel myself beginning to tear.

My heart is being ripped apart
By doubts I could once never have imagined.
How did I *ever* get to *this* place?
It's so hard for me to fathom.

Pain is stealing all the joy in my life;
Now it seems all I have left are tears.
Memories of bountiful blessings of the past
Are fading with each passing year.

What would You have me to do, Lord?
Where would You have me to go?
I wait here in desperation;
Please, Lord, I just need to know!

I can take some pills to ease some of the pain
As I wait for Your Will to be done,
But in the dead of night, fear hisses to me
That the healing may never come.

My prayers have been ceaseless;
Not one day has ever past
When I have not made supplication,
But *how long* must prayers last?

I pray for myself,
Others pray for me,
Yet no relief comes;
Is it *ever* to be?

The Spirit of The Father
Is attuned to His child's cry.
He Sees the desert place piled high with doubts;
He Hears the moaning and the sighs.

"My child, I Have Heard *every* prayer
That you have ever said to Me.
It is time to "lift the veil,"
For your eyes to fully see.

"I love to Hear your prayers,
To Know you seek My Face,
But there comes a time when asking
Must find a "resting place."

"In this time of in-between,
Before Faith holds healing's hand,
May you wait in *anticipation*
Of the unfolding of My Divine Plan.

"In this time of in-between,
Before manifestation has taken place,
Wait within the Silence;
You will sense My Mercy and My Grace.

"I Long to Hear your thankfulness
Despite what circumstances may seem.
You have asked, and it has been Given;
Look for visions within your dreams.

"Thank Me with each new day
That *your healing has been done;*
Thank Me with unshakeable assurance
That *the victory has been won!*

"The enemy wants to fill this time
With *all* that he can bring,
To kill, to steal, and to destroy
All the praises that you sing.

"*Sing,* My Child, *sing*!
Despite your failing flesh,
Sing, My Child, *sing*!
It is *then* you will be blessed!

"Offer praises and thankfulness
Though all may seem the same.
Remember what I have shown to you;
Remember the reason for which I Came.

"I showed you through My Own Suffering
That trials will *surely* come.
You will always have some challenges
Until your life on earth is done.

"Yet when you meet each struggle
With a trust that *can not* be shaken,
The fire of faith is re-kindled;
From your sleep of deception you awaken.

"Turn your focus from the flesh
To rise above what you may feel;
When you place your eyes on Me,
You will know that which is *truly* real.

"Lay your supplications down;
Trust Me and *believe*.
I Am The Great I Am;
I Am *all* you will ever need."

Romans 4:20–25
Romans 5:1–5

December 2011

Background of "The Time In-Between"

A friend had been going through some severe health challenges for well over a year. The medical profession had told him that pills to control the pain was all that could be done, but all the pills were doing was causing side effects. After months of prayer, nothing had changed. It seemed that an answer was not to be. This poem is the Lord's response to this person's desperate cry (as well as the universal cry of each of us in our own personal trials). It speaks to the in-between time, when we find ourselves sinking under the weight of doubt with seemingly no help in sight until we realize that *He is all we will ever need to overcome every struggle on this earth*. Time belongs to Him, and healing is in His hands. As we place our trust in Him, we find the peace and rest we seek in order to pass through all trials.

The Burden-Lifter

Father, The things that once held substance
Are slipping from my grasp.
So many trials bombard me;
I am just too tired to ask.

To call upon Your Name,
To ask You to please hear,
To ask that through it all
You will always remain near,

To ask You for a sign,
To hope it will appear,
To try to find my path's direction,
To ask that it be clear.

Now all I have is anxiety;
I grow so weary of the wait.
Eternity seems an impossibility
As I lose sight of Heaven's Gate.

My flesh is taking over.
My spirit growing dim.
It seems the battle is over;
There is no strength left in me to win.

How could I have come this far,
For now I am so weak?
I remember times of victory
When I stood on mountain peaks.

I never thought of worry,
For my trust was *all* in You.
I knew no matter *what* would come,
You would *always* see me through.

Father, As I think of all the things
You have done for me in the past,
I am coming to a realization:
I realize I didn't always ask.

Faith like a child is what I had;
I never thought to question.
I looked to *You* in *all* I did;
I followed *Your* Direction.

I knew Your Purpose for my life
Was to have all that is good.
Just as a loving father,
You did all that You could.

So, as a child, I return to You, Jesus;
I lay down *all* my concerns,
For on this journey that You Walk with me,
There is one thing I have learned.

You Told me, "Lay your burdens down, My child,
I Will Carry them for you."
Thank You for this remembrance,
For *all* Your Promises are true.

You are The Burden-Lifter;
I have *no* load to bear.
Your Love for me is endless;
You Are with me *everywhere*.

When anxious questions rumble within my soul,
When no answers can be retrieved,
I release *all* my fears and rest in You
As I remember I need only to *believe*.

Deuteronomy 31:6
Psalm 139: 23–24
Proverbs 15:15
1 Peter 5:7

December 2011

Note on "The Burden-Lifter"

This poem goes from the depths of despair to a renewal of joy as burdens are released. Remembering what it is to have the faith of a child, a child who trusts their parent unconditionally, we feel the tremendous love our heavenly Father has for each of us. He is there to free us from anxiety, to renew our strength, to evaporate our fear. Suddenly, we realize we have nothing left to carry, for He has taken it all within His hands the moment we said, "I believe in You, Jesus!"

The Coming

Thinking about this world,
Pondering the darkness of its night,
Trying to find some kind of hope,
A tiny flicker of any light,

Looking all around,
Seeking from side to side,
So much that's seen is torment
Built from Satan's lies

Suffocating pain and sorrow,
Families torn apart,
Lives filled with empty spaces,
Stony places once called hearts.

If one's search for happiness
Causes them to break a trust,
They think they have no other choice;
It is *their* life, and they *must*.

What about the children
Who love their mother and their father?
Formed into a family,
Yet now their parents say, "Why bother?"

Circumstances cloaked in grief,
Joy? It cannot even be comprehended.
Is this the substance of a life
Until its time on earth is ended?

Living aimlessly from day to day,
Without rhyme and without reason,
Deadened lives buried in a desert place,
Dragging through each scorching season.

Thoughts so wrapped up inside oneself,
There is no room to think of another.
So many burdens to push and pull along,
Who can worry about their sister or brother?

Morals turned into murky mire,
Thoughts so twisted and so tattered,
Destruction of love that once was so precious,
The death of so much that had mattered.

Perversion running rampant
Through thoughtless words and deeds,
No consideration of consequences,
The planting of rotten seeds.

Voices of delusion
Determining the false to be what's true,
Lies carried to fruition,
The path of destruction is walked through.

Integrity shattered in pieces,
Love? A thing of the past.
Nothing left to hold onto,
How long can this nothingness last?

Discouragement, despair, and destruction,
That is all that will remain.
Lord! We need a miracle in this desert!
Won't You *please* send your Healing rain?

His message from Eternity
Flows forth from within the lines.
A Voice of Thunder filled with wrath yet filled with Love,
The Creator of All Time:

"Satan, father of deceit!
Your time is at an end.
My warring angels are gathering
As your *final* days you spend.

"You came to kill, to steal and destroy
All goodness in My Creation.
The evil that you spew out
Is reaching its duration.

"In your frenzy to annihilate
All that I Have Given,
You have deluded yourself to be victorious.
Have you forgotten? *I Have Risen!*

I Promised to return
To this world I have made;
It is too late for you to plead mercy.
My Hand will *not* be stayed!

"In days of soon-to-come,
My Signs and Wonders will unfold.
There is *nothing* to compare them to;
These things have *never* been seen nor told.

"My Judgment will crash down,
Smashing all boulders in its path.
You have yet to see My fury;
Now you will see the full force of My wrath.

"For those who choose to follow Me
Even at the last,
I will pour out My Love and Mercy;
I will forgive *all* that is past.

"For their paths were filled with darkness,
Their eyes too blind to see.
You stole from them their vision;
You pulled their sight from Me.

"They have read of Me and heard of Me,
Yet so many do not believe.
They will now see My Works as evidence;
They will *know* they have been deceived.

I Am the Lamb Who was Slain;
I Am The King of Kings.
My Return is drawing *imminent*
As the Praises of Heaven ring.

Revelation 2:11
Revelation 3:11
Revelation 11:15–19
Revelation 16:15
Revelation 22:7
Revelation 22:12
Revelation 22:20

December 2011

Note on "The Coming"

Through the poems in this book, a recurring theme has been the intensifying supernatural battle raging upon the earth, the urgency of taking a stand as a follower of Jesus Christ, the emphasis that His Return is imminent. "The Coming" is one more confirmation as He express His fury that will be unleashed upon the enemy and yet the mercy He will extend until the very end upon those whose hearts are opened to Him.

Lord, My life is at a crossroads;
I'm not sure which path to take.
I come to You for answers;
I *don't* want to make a mistake.

On this journey I have traveled,
There have been so many ups and downs.
Sometimes I have felt like "flying,"
At others I have been *glued* onto the ground.

When I have followed Your Direction,
You have always let me see
That what You have Provided
Is the *perfect* choice for me.

Though to my own eyes it may make no sense,
It may grate upon my flesh,
When I hear "Come this way" From The Stillness within,
"This way" always proves to be the best.

From Your Spirit Flows assurance;
Anxiety has *nothing* to do with You.
Whatever river I need to cross,
You Will *always* See me through.

Through the flood of my emotions,
When I feel like I am sinking,
You Are my life's Preserver;
You Know just what I'm thinking.

So as I ponder what to do,
I *know* I am not alone.
You Have proven Your Love and Care for me
In all that I have known.

When my thought-waves crashed around me,
When I could take no more,
I cried out to You to Help me;
You Guided me to the Peaceful Shore.

In times of grief, When loved ones went on,
I felt the brush of angel's wings.
You Held me *so* close; Your Presence was *Profound*.
I knew someday my heart would once more sing.

You Opened my eyes to Your Truth that abides
No matter *what* circumstances may be.
You Healed my blindness; You Brought in Your Light.
I was once again able to see,

To see and to fly and to rise high above
Any pain, any guilt, any shame.
With my sight stayed on *You*, my course is defined;
I have no one and nothing to blame.

Things are as they are, but when I look at the stars,
I know there is *so much more.*
You Are The Creator of Good; Your Hand Moves the earth.
It is *You* I am living for.

You *knew* before I came to be
That I would some day be in *this* place;
You *knew* that in *this* moment
I would come to seek Your Face.

So, my Jesus, As I ask for *Your* Direction,
What is the path *You* Have for me?
I *hear* Your Whisper within the stillness:
"My child, The *best* is yet to be."

Matthew 7:7

January 2012

Background of "Seeking"

Someone very close to me had suffered a devastating event in her marriage. She didn't believe she would ever be able to trust again, to love again, to feel secure again. Her world had been turned upside down, and she felt as if she were falling off. The Lord gave me this poem for her, to give her assurance and direction, to draw her eyes to look upon the hope held within His hands for her, to show her that *His* light was shining into her future and that she had nothing to fear—and neither do you.

Wait and listen within the calm;
Hear the rustle of angels' wings.
Wait and listen within the storms;
You will hear angels sweetly sing,

"Yes, My child,

"Within your visions covered in clouds,
My rays of sunshine wait.
Seasons change, the winds blow fiercely,
But by *My Choice*, not a mistake.

"*Trust and wait* within My Timing;
All is in My Hands.
The fulfillment of *your* heart's desires
Resides within *My* Eternal Plan.

"I have not Called you to have come so far
To now leave you alone.
Trust Me, My child, Your steps are secure;
I will use the seeds that have been sown.

"When it seems as if nothing is happening,
When all that has been done appears to be lost,
My Glory will burst forth as the Springtime,
Resurrection after the deepest frost.

"So let sadness melt away
Within the warmth of My Limitless Love.
I have Seen *all* that has been done below;
I have guided *all* from Above.

"For My Plans to reach fulfillment,
Familiarity *must* give way to change
For the lost to come to know Me,
To know *the reason* why I Came.

"My good and faithful servant,
You have placed your heart in Mine.
I Am with you in this moment;
I Am with you through *all* time.

"You have selflessly surrendered
The ways of the world's pleasures;
When you chose the higher road,
You became My *Precious* Treasure.

"Since I Called you as My disciple,
You have followed with your humble heart;
Through the stumbling, through the torments,
We have *never* been apart.

"Your humble, loving heart
Would be a feast in the demon's lair.
Discouragement, despair, disillusionment
Are the bait with which to snare.

"You are the shepherd of *My* people;
You are *My* reflection on the earth.
You are *My* good and faithful servant;
In *Me*, You have found your worth.

"I Am Giving you a deeper *discernment*;
I Am intensifying the fire of *boldness*.
I Am doing *a new thing* in you;
I Am bringing you to *wholeness*.

"Waste not *one* more moment in fear, My child,
When you hear the demons at your door.
With the strength I Am instilling in you,
They *cannot* harm you any more.

"*Rest* within these words,
For they are *surely* meant for you.
You have *known* Me as your Father;
You have *known* Me to be True.

"The Son of Victory Is on the horizon
Just below the hills.
You will *see* the Light of Dawn breaking
In those times when you are still.

"You are my faithful servant;
You have done what I have Asked.
Though the way has not been easy,
You have taken on the task.

"I joined two together
For My Work that must be done.
Through *unity* of vision,
The victory *will* be won.

"Two vessels, each so different
Yet joined as *one* within my plan,
Two vessels sharing the same Love
Within the Heart of the Great I Am.

"Fear *not*, My Faithful Children,
Continue following *boldly* in My Steps.
Great harvest is about to come;
The appointed time since the beginning
has been set.

Revelation 3:7–10

January 2012

Background of "Faithfulness"

This poem was written for my pastor and his wife, awesome vessels of the Lord. They "walk out" the words of the Bible. They live according to the example of Jesus, and they draw others to do the same. Their journey has not been easy, but they have persevered in their mission for Him, to seek and save the lost. I see "Faithfulness" as a beautiful representation of the Lord's thankfulness and appreciation pouring out into verse for each of them and for *all* other shepherds who have persevered, walking in integrity and remaining steadfast in the Truth.

Looking Through the Lattice

A stifling blanket of suffocation
Shuts out the light within this world,
Tucked taut around the edges,
Smothering any words of hope that might be heard.

Darkness, blackness, never-ending night in the soul,
This is all there *seems* to be.
But oh, My child, These are just appearances;
They have *nothing* to do with *Me*.

On the surface, there is darkness,
Yet look *deeper*; You will see
The flicker of a candle,
The Coming Light that is to Be.

I Am your Reality;
In Me there is only Light.
I Am your Love, your Peace, your Joy;
I Am the clarity in your sight.

The road has *never* been easy
For those who have heard My Call,
But this you shall *never* doubt:
I Am with you through it *all*.

Down through the ages, on and on,
With My suffering saints I have Walked
When they have been slandered, persecuted, left to die,
When they have been ridiculed, when they have been mocked.

Do you see yourself within this picture, My child?
Are you experiencing *this* today?
Are you beginning to doubt that I have Heard your knock?
Are you beginning to lose your way?

Remember Me as the blazing Pillar of Fire;
Remember Me as the Cloud of Preservation hovering above.
Remember Me as I was in the desert;
Remember Me as Never-Ending Love.

Within the seeds planted in richest soil,
The *greatest* harvest will surely come.
There is no room for doubt within these perfectly-planted rows;
Satan *cannot* destroy the work that has already been done.

I Am with you as you labor
To draw *many* within My Fold.
I Am The Good and Everlasting Shepherd;
My sheep I Will *forever* Hold.

I Am Calling My ministering, warring angels
To protect *all* of My pastures
As the wolves of Satan lurk and howl outside the hedge,
They will *not* get what they are after.

The time of easy access
Has come to its determined end;
Fearless faith will see its full reward.
Deception and evil, the withering wrath that
I *Will* Send.

There will be *no* further doubts
As to Who this world Belongs.
It was created by My Hand;
It will return to Me with *your* songs.

Sing on, My Children!
Let your Praises *ring!*
Sing on in Praise and Thankfulness
For the Glories I Am about to Bring.

I Am drawing *ever* Closer;
Heaven and earth are about to collide.
Wait, watch, listen;
In Me continue *ever* to abide.

When you stop within the stillness,
When you listen with your heart,
You will hear My gentle Whisper;
You will *know* we have *never* been apart.

I Am Looking through the lattice;
I see *each* of your plights.
I Am Looking through the lattice;
You have *never* left My Sight.

Song of Solomon 2:9

February 2012

Background of "Looking Through The Lattice"

I never know when the Lord will choose to send a message; each has been totally unexpected, each cherished beyond words. And so it was on this Valentine's Day early morning. I see "Looking Through the Lattice" as a love letter from Him, pouring out His encouragement through the deep river of love that flows from His heart into ours. It is a message of realization as to how close He truly is as He watches through the lattice. The Father of Forever watches over His precious children, waiting for each one to rest within His gaze.

Shelter

Blackness is all around me
As I stumble through endless nights.
My afflictions loom like mighty mountains;
I think I may die from fright.

Fiery darts of doubt and deep depression
Hitting the center of my heart,
How many wounds can a heart endure
Before it shatters and falls apart?

Feelings of peace and happiness
Now seem like such an illusion
Will the remainder of my days drag out in desperation
Until they slam shut with an empty conclusion?

My loved ones buried in burdens,
What can I do, and what can I say?
How can I lift them up in their trials?
Father, There *must* be a way!

Lord, where are You?
You had brought me out of the mire!
Will You now leave me here in this darkness,
My faith burning to ashes on this funeral pyre?

Rays of sunshine once filled my life
As I came to know Your Ways.
I *knew* The Presence of Your Love;
You Gave The Purpose to my days.

But where are You *now*, Lord?
Please don't leave me here!
In my struggles, I strive to sense Your Touch;
I need to know that you are near!

Waiting within the deafening stillness,
Seconds ticking by,
I *suddenly* hear His Gentle Whisper
As He crushes Satan's lies:

"My child, Listen to *My* Voice Now.
Your search for strength, it is in vain.
Remember Who I Am;
Remember Why I Came.

"*You* have no strength within yourself
To withstand the trials of this earth.
I Am your Strength and your Sustainer;
It is *in Me* you find *your* worth.

"You are drowning in deception
In the flood of Satan's filth.
His goal is to destroy you;
You have known this from the first.

"He is blinding you with fear
So you lose your sight of Me.
While you remain focused on his torment,
You will have no clarity to *see,*

"To *see* that I Am with you,
To *know* that I Have *never* left your side,
To *hold onto* My Words of Promise,
To *continue* in My Strength to Abide.

"*I Have Overcome it all*, My Child;
You have *nothing* left to fear.
Remain within My Word,
Then your pathway will be cleared.

"*Rest* in our relationship,
In the bond you have come to know.
You are My Precious Child;
I will *never* let you go.

"I Love you with an *endless* Love,
Which cannot be expressed in words.
Echoing throughout Eternity,
It is a song that is *Ever-Heard.*

"*Rest*, My Child, *Rest;*
Leave your loved ones in My Care
Each one of them belongs to *Me*;
My Love for them is *beyond* compare.

"*Remember* what I Have Done for you
In days that have now past.
For in your remembering, you will see
That today's torments *will not last.*

"My Love is what sustained you *then*,
As so it will be *now.*
You have *no need* to worry;
You have *no need* to know when or how.

"I Am the Devine Designer
Of *all* that will come to pass.
All things *will* work together for Good
As you abide in Me until the last.

"In the world there is *much* suffering,
But I Have Overcome.
I Am the Defeater of the demonic;
The Victory *has* been won.

"I Am the Refuge for your soul;
Rest within My Arms.
It is *here* you will find Peace and Comfort;
Here, you are protected from *all* harm.

"I Am your Shelter from *all* storms;
Through My Spirit, *all* victories are won.
I Am The Great I Am;
My Kingdom is soon to Come.

"Let My Peace pervade your spirit *now*;
Calm yourself to *see*
That *everything* you will ever need
Will *forever* be found in *Me*."

Romans 8:28
Romans 8:37

March 2012

Background of "Shelter"

I noted a few months ago that there had been a shift in the writing of the poems. I find that many times, they are now "impressed" in my spirit to be given to a particular person. Sometimes I know them personally, and sometimes the poem has been drawn from a prayer request for someone I've never met. The poem "Shelter" was written to be given to a friend of mine who is going through a time of extreme trial and suffering, a devastating event had happened regarding one of her daughters, another child had just moved away with the two grandchildren, and a close friend had just been involved in an accident. The Lord reaches out to her in the words of this poem to assure her of His *continual* love and care for her, as well as for all her loved ones, to assure her that she can *rest,* that she is *sheltered,* that she is forever His precious child—just as *you* are.

The Unexpected

I was going through my days
Never expecting you to come,
But suddenly you were there,
A seed of life begun.

My heart was filled with happiness,
Imagining what was to be
As I pondered the precious treasure
Growing inside of me.

I pictured the faces of family
As we would tell them of our joy.
Would we dream of pink or blue?
Would you be a girl or boy?

So recently we had felt the loss
Of a loved one who had slipped away;
Your coming was like a morning star,
Shining in the dawn of a new day.

Then, just as suddenly as you had come,
In an instant you were gone.
Yet My thoughts of you are lingering
Like the melody of a sad, sad song.

I cry my tears within the night;
I ask You, God, *Oh why?*
Why did You Cause a life to begin,
Only to have it die?

The Father's Tears are Falling
As He Hears His Child's plea.
He *Longs* to Heal her pain;
He *Longs* for her to *see* as He Would *see.*

His Words Whisper in the stillness:

"My Child, *all* things work together for Good
For those whose hearts are Mine.
Though today you see no reason,
You will see it over time.

"Look back upon what has already been;
Have you not seen My Hand Sustain?
In your joy and in your sadness,
In times of sunshine as well as rain?

"Through *all* your seasons *I Will Be*
As you walk upon this earth.
I Will Love you and Uplift you;
I Will Show you your *true* worth.

"*You* are My priceless treasure
Held within My Heart,
Within the *same* place I Hold the child
From whom you had to part.

"Once I Breathe the breath of life
Into the flesh of man,
Though the body fails, the spirit lives on.
This is My Eternal Plan.

"I Will Use this separation you have suffered
To draw others unto Me.
Through *your* words they will sense *My* Presence,
Through *your* loss they will begin to *see*,

"To *see* that I Will Guide them
Through *every* storm that they may face,
To *see* that I Will Hold them
Within My Love and in My Grace.

"Where once they felt such hopelessness,
Through your eyes they will begin to see
That in *each* and *every* circumstance,
They can place their trust *In Me*.

"The steps you have walked
Through this journey of pain
Will be used for *My Glory*;
They will *not* be in vain.

"Trust Me in your trials;
Trust Me in *all* things.
Lay your heart within My Hands;
You will *have* The Peace I Bring."

Psalm 147:3

April 2012

Background of "The Unexpected"

I had met a young woman who was overjoyed to find that she was pregnant. She started taking her prenatal vitamins and had an ultrasound done in hopes of seeing her little one. Sadly, within a few days of telling me, she had suffered a miscarriage, and she was left with the question, *why?* and the pain of thinking about what could have been. This woman's beloved grandmother had passed away four months before; this baby would have brought much happiness into a grieving family. Why had sadness been the result instead? A few days had passed when she told me she had gone on the internet to try and find a poem that might reflect something of what she was feeling about her baby. She felt that it would serve as a memory of her little one, something to speak to the fact that the baby had been here, if only for a little while. As she was speaking, I knew within my spirit that the Lord was going to send a poem just for *her* and what *she* had gone through and yet also for so many others who had endured the same situation. You see, as God would have it, she was working at a pregnancy clinic. And, as God would have it, she was given a poem, "The Unexpected."

Reflections of Creation

A cloudless canopy of deepest blue;
Gentle wind whispering through the trees;
Bunches of birds united in song,
Their chirps lilting upon the soft breeze;

Fields of flowers burst into bloom,
Each petal painted unique;
A carousel of colors swirling around;
A treasure chest for every artist who seeks;

Lacey leaves on bending boughs,
In shades of every green;
How long have these trees stood through time?
How much they must have seen.

Ripples on the river; Ducks skimming the surface,
Searching for a spot to "sit;"
A silvery slice of a fish breaks through the water,
Then splashes back with a quick flip.

A panorama of pastures stretches across the horizon;
For miles and miles they go on.
Empty of evidence of man's fingerprints;
It is The Creator to whom they belong.

As I wait in silence,
Gazing upon this scene,
My soul drinks in its beauty,
Refreshed by the reality of *all* it means.

Nature, A piece of Heaven
The Lord Has Placed before our eyes.
If we *truly* saw what is before us,
Revelation would *crush* the devil's lies.

For how can we doubt a Creator
Who Has Reached down from above
To *fill* our world with beauty
Through which He Tries to Show His Love?

More than Love, His *Very* Presence
Surrounds and Lives within all we see;
His Creation *Shouts* his Glory.
It is there for *all* to see.

Still we stumble on in blindness,
Smothered in the skepticism of the world's ways,
Imagining we in ourselves can create something lasting
As we struggle through our days.

Yet as I look upon The Face of God
On this balmy, beautiful day,
I see The *Truth* without any questions;
There are *no* shades of gray.

The answer is as crystal-clear
As the blue sky high above.
He Created the hand that writes this,
And I was created within His Love.

All He Asks is that I *return* the Love
That He Instilled in me,
Treating others as *I* would want to be treated,
Relying on *Him* to see,

To see that *anything* that I may do
Within this life of mine
Is meant to reflect His Being,
The Father of All Time.

The Creator of all in Nature,
The Creator of *each* breath of *each* human being,
The Creator of selfless Love hung upon a Cross,
The Creator Who Gives life its meaning.

As I bring this poem to a close,
I think about what it would be
To live in a world *without* Nature.
What would there be to see?

Darkness with no sunlight,
Silence without birds' songs,
Blackness with no colors,
Just desert places going *on* and *on* and *on*.

Thank You for Your Love, Lord,
And for *all* that You Keep Giving.
Open our eyes to see Your Face,
And may our Thanksgiving be reflected in our living.

Psalm 24:1

April 2012

Background of "Reflections of Creation"

This poem was written on a spring day in the California Delta area, at the same location where the very first poem was given in January 2009. The date this was written has a special significance because it is the birthday of my friend Lisa. The theme of the poem is also meaningful as it relates to Lisa because one of my most special memories of being with her is as follows:

I had given her a ride to the bus stop one early morning. As I dropped her off, I heard her say, "Well, thank you!" and I realized she wasn't talking to me. She was talking to her Father, the Creator of the universe, as she looked at the picture He was painting across the sky, in a mixture of colors only *He* could blend, heralding the dawn of a new day. It was a precious moment for me. I truly *sensed* the Lord *listening* to these heartfelt words from His beloved Lisa. I believe this poem is His gift and response to her on her birthday, His "Your welcome, Lisa; it has touched My heart that you are one who truly sees My face in *all* that I provide."

The Potter's Tears

The Potter's Tears are Falling
Upon the broken vessel at His Feet.
He *Longs* to make it whole again,
To See it as complete.

He Had Created this container,
Once *so* beautiful to behold,
A priceless, timeless treasure,
More precious than pure gold.

Wrapped within an angel's wings,
The vessel of a child had arrived upon this earth
Protectively packaged in clouds of innocence,
A *mighty* miracle revealed through birth.

A child filled up to the brim
With the essence of pure Love
Yet untainted from this world's cares,
A vessel formed from Hands above.

But as earthly days unfolded,
Time here slowly took its toll.
Hurts began hammering upon the vessel,
Forming chips and cracks and holes.

The angry words of parents,
The betrayal by a friend,
A commitment shattered by lies,
A marriage coming to an end;

So *many* thoughtless actions,
So *many* wounding words,
Love's contents slowly seeping out,
Drip, drip, drip, it could be heard.

Then that day arrived
When the vessel could finally hold no more;
Cracked by deep addictions, traumas, regrets,
The contents of love spilled out upon the floor.

Shattered in so many pieces,
Appearing damaged beyond repair,
Useless rubble upon the ground,
And no one seemed to care.

But The Potter Who Had Created
The beautiful vessel that had once been
Places His Healing Hands upon the pieces,
Beginning to form them once again.

He Gently Reaches for one piece,
Then He Picks another up.
He joins them back together
With the bond of Faith and Trust.

He so carefully forms the shape
Of *each* and *every* part,
And when He stops to Gaze at it,
He Sees the beauty of the heart.

His Voice Softly Speaks,

"Now, My Child, you are ready to be filled;
You have been *sealed* within My Word.
The truth has set you *free;*
My Voice you have now heard.

"Though your life's surface is still dented
And the cracks may still be seen,
You are *now* My vessel who tells a story
Of Heaven's Hope and destined dreams.

"I now place you in the kiln
Of My Holy Spirit's Fire.
You are My Precious vessel;
You are My Heart's Desire.

"You have given Me your life;
Now we are as One.
The devil's plot to destroy has been defeated;
The victory has been won."

Now As He Gazes at His vessel
That has the sheen of glistening gold,
The Potter's Face is Reflected, as in a mirror,
With a Smile that is beautiful to behold.

Ephesians 1:7

May 2012

Note on "The Potter's Tears"

"The Potter's Tears" is the only poem that has come in sections, with a space of several months between completion. Begun in December 2011, it was not completed until May 2012. I can only explain it as being within the timing of the Lord. It expresses His immense love for each of us, no matter *what* our condition, no matter how broken or shattered. *His* vision is always to see us as complete. Though *we* may have given up on ourselves, *He* never will. "The Potter's Tears" speaks to the fact that *each* one of us *is* redeemable. All we need to do is give our lives to Him *completely* and *rest* within His hands. He will restore the broken pieces and mend the broken places. The "dented" parts of our past, which we had once thought to be so devastating, will be used as declarations that *all* of His promises are true. He is the great Restorer of *any* broken life.

The essence of believing,
The strength to hold on tight,
The power to press through fear,
The facing of shadows in the night,

The cord that connects the things on earth
To those that are above,
The *resting* Place in His Sacred Heart,
That Place of Enduring Love,

Within the fiery torments,
Through prolonged persecutions and testing trials,
The saints of ages past stood *firm*;
They rebuked *all* doubt and shunned denials.

Their eyes of Faith looked *not* on circumstance;
They were gripped upon the Cross,
That symbol of pain and suffering,
The picture of the price of what Faith costs.

For Jesus *never* Said to believe
Was an *easy* thing to do,
Rather He Said, "Take up your cross and follow Me;"
He Stated what was true.

As a boat that sails smoothly
On waters that look like glass,
Our faith is so easy to control
When we have all that we ask.

But when the tempest winds of trials
Begin blowing with hurricane force,
The journey suddenly becomes perilous,
So *hard* to stay the course.

It is *there* that Satan lurks,
Waiting to grip the direction of our life.
He knows his greatest opportunity
Is when we suffer pain and strife.

When doubts begin to seep through ruptures
Within the broken vessel of our mind,
When question crashes against question,
When *no* safe harbor of answers can we find,

Satan hisses to his demons,
"*Now* is our chance to win!
This once faith-filled believer
Will now fall right into sin!

"His doubts will overcome him;
Let's grab this chance and flee!
Let's finish burning his faith to ashes,
Then he will belong to *Me!*"

Yet, through a crack in the deception,
There is a glimmer of a Light,
Enough to begin breaking
Into the darkness of this night.

As doubting eyes are opened
To the reality of the scheme,
The cry rings out, "*Get behind me, Satan;*
Your wicked ways have *all* been seen!"

Remembrance of precious Words
Of our Savior and our Master:
"Leave *now*, devil of deceit,
You will *not* get what you are after."

Suddenly, Peace falls like a blanket.
There is joy beyond compare
As The Voice of Jesus is clearly heard,
Filling the stillness in the air.

"Oh, My child,

"As *I* have gone through suffering,
So suffering *you*, too, must endure.
I have Told you there will be perils,
Yet it seems you have not yet heard.

"Seasons come and seasons go;
Life does *not* remain the same.
Faith *must* flow in all times,
No matter *what* the change.

"Delivery from the demonic,
Strength to rise above all pain,
When you *stand* upon The Rock,
These victories *will* be gained.

Your Faith is your strong fortress,
Covered with The Shadow of My Wings.
Rest within this shelter;
You will *find* the joy it brings.

2 Samuel 22:2

May 2012

I Note on "The Fortress"

I believe that having received this poem near the end of this book is significant. It represents the melody of the chord of faith, the connection that brings all the verses of all the poems together in one crescendo. Faith is the beginning and the end of our journey and everything in-between. "Come, follow Me," He said, and so we step out in faith. Throughout the verses of the poems, we hear His voice: *"Trust Me; have faith in Me. I will not disappoint you."* As we read this poem, He guides us to rest, *rest within the fortress of faith,* under the shadow of the wings of the Message Maker, our Lord and Savior, Jesus Christ. *To you be all the honor and glory, Jesus, forever and ever, amen.*

As I think about The Savior,
There is nothing to compare
With the Mercy He *Longs* to Show,
With the Love He Has to Share.

Mercy and love? You question.
Surely *not* for *me*.
If He Sees what *I* am doing and have done,
From me He Will *surely* flee.

Yet this is just another
Of Satan's lurid lies
To keep you far from calling
Upon The One Who Offers Life.

Jesus *longs* to Hold you close,
To draw you to His Heart.
It was *never* His intention
That you should *ever* live apart.

No matter *where* you have been,
No matter *what* you have done,
You are His precious daughter;
You are His longed-for son.

He Looks at you with Eyes of Love,
Not with guilt and condemnation.
He is *not* an accuser,
For *His* Joy is within *your* salvation.

You have been *Washed* in His Blood,
Covered with His Grace,
Cleansed, and *forgiven*.
For you, in Eternity There is a Place.

When you feel that no one understands
The emotions you are feeling,
Listen for His Whisper,
For by your side He Is *surely* kneeling,

Waiting For you to hear His Voice,
Waiting For you to feel His Healing Touch,
Waiting For you to rest and realize
No one will ever Love you as much

As Him.

Jesus, the Lamb Who was Slain:
He Came to Seek and Save the lost.
For Himself, He was given nothing,
Yet for you, He Paid the ultimate cost.

John 3:16

June 2012

Note on "For You"

As I contemplate what this poem means to me, I think about the *enormity* of the love of Jesus, the love He extends, not just to a select few but to each and every human being ever created. This poem was written *for you;* He is speaking *to you,* and He longs to share His heart *with you.* He is waiting for *you* to accept Him.

The Crossroads

Father, My life is at a crossroads;
I don't know which way to go.
My heart quakes with confusion;
You *have* to let me know.

Looking to the left,
I see the sign marked "happiness."
You *Said* within Your Word
That for my life, You Want the best.

At the beginning of this path,
I can see the sun is shining.
So long enveloped in dark storm clouds,
Now I can see a silver lining.

I *know* this is the one for me;
I feel so self-assured.
Thank You for Your Guidance, Lord;
I *know* my voice You Have Heard!

I see the road is smooth ahead;
There is nothing in the way.
My steps will be secure
As I walk through carefree days.

I know there is the "other" road,
And I'd like to turn to see,
But my soul is so determined
This is the one true path for me.

I have nothing to carry with me;
My travel will be light.
All that I have held onto
I left behind last night.

And so, Filled with anticipation,
This traveler of life takes flight.
Running through the trees,
They have soon been lost from sight.

At the beginning of the other road,
There has been Someone Standing.
He Has Heard every thought of the traveler;
He Has Known each step that they were planning.

The Eyes of Jesus are Filled with sadness
As tears stream down His Holy Face,
For this traveler, once His faithful follower,
Has now been *lost* within that place.

His Gentle Voice Speaks within the stillness,

"My child,

"The fires burning in your flesh
Have destroyed the fortress of your faith.
You do not yet realize that you have fled
From the place where you were *safe*.

"You have run into the devil's lair,
Lured by deceptive light.
All too soon you will be devoured
In the darkness of his pitch-black night.

"He has deceived you into thinking
You have found 'direction' within My Word.
No, My deafened child,
It has not been My Voice you have heard.

"True, I Came to bring you joy
In abundance, overflowing,
But the River's Source is My Holy Spirit,
Not the flesh-way of *your* knowing.

"You say that you are self-assured,
In this, too, you have accepted Satan's bait,
For in relying on your*self,*
You have closed the Heavenly Gate.

"Yes, Your travel will be lighter
As you start on this downward path,
For you have left behind integrity
And all the other things I Have Asked.

"You say the road you have chosen
Has no obstacles you can see.
So true, For those who choose the path to *Me*
Choose the road to Calvary.

"There are boulders and there are deserts;
There are dry and torrid times.
Yet At the ending of their journey,
It is Eternity My Followers will find.

"For *you,* Should you choose to continue down this road
To the finality of your days,
You will find the specter of death waiting at its ending;
Too late you will see the price that you have paid.

"Had you turned to look and see
The road where I was waiting,
You would have seen the sign marked "*Truth,*"
The place where there is *no* hesitating.

"For *Truth* is pure-white clarity;
There are *no* shades of gray.
*My Word is Everlasting;
I Am The Life, The Way.*

"I Am The God of *Truth;*
There are *no* 'buts' within My Word.
My Voice is *clearly* Written,
Yet still you have *not* heard.

"Unconditional Love that is Everlasting,
Solid, and Secure,
Remember all that we have been through;
Remember all that *I* have helped you endure.

"My Mercy is Eternal;
I Will *continually* Call you back toward Home.
My Arms wait here, Extended,
To enfold you once again in My Love that you have known.

"Time is growing short;
You have *no room* to wait.
My Return is drawing *imminent*,
When My True Followers I Will Take."

1 John 5:6–13

June 2012

Note on "The Crossroads"

In this particular poem, the verses kept surging through my spirit with a seldom-experienced sense of urgency.

The message is unmistakable: no matter what our human tendencies might devise to satisfy the longings of our flesh, God's Word *cannot* and *will not* be twisted. No matter what we might try to say or do to justify taking the "wide road," no matter how entitled we might feel because of all that we've been through, our companion on this road will not be Jesus. The road He walked Himself was *narrow,* strewn with suffering. His suffering culminated in a death so agonizing that we cannot even begin to comprehend the magnitude of His pain. He endured *all* as a *spotless* Lamb, entitled to *everything* as the King of Kings, and yet He claimed *nothing.* He compromised *nothing.* He came to show His love for us; He came to die for us; He came for us so that we might have eternal life with Him. He clearly mapped out the path for us to follow; He did not provide any alternate routes because there are *none.* He *clearly* defined the Way of *Truth*, and it points *directly* to *Him.*

Higher Ground

I see her every Sunday,
His Glow upon her face.
She comes to His House to worship,
To praise Him in this place.

Wearing colors bright as sunshine,
Reminding me of Spring,
She has walked within the Winter;
She *knows* full-well what trials bring.

Her voice is soft and gentle,
With no harshness to be found.
Her steps are slow yet so secure
As she walks on *solid, higher* ground.

When I look into *her* eyes,
I see *His* Light of Love.
Serenity in sight beyond,
Focused on things above.

Her Knight in shining armor
Walks *continually* by her side.
Fear is flung far from her
As her Jesus Protects, Consoles, Abides.

Trust with no conditions,
They walk on Hand in hand.
Despite worldly words of hopelessness spoken,
Her life *rests* in The Arms of The Great I AM.

Faith, Hope, Love,
Overflowing beyond all measure,
Knowing the joy of Jesus' Promise,
She has found His offered Treasure.

A *miracle* among us,
Yet do I have the eyes to see
That the trust within *this* woman
Should also be found in *me?*

Father, When the storm clouds gather over *me,*
When *I* am pelted with "torrential rain,"
Please keep *me* on the path where Debbie walks,
The *higher ground*, where all is gained.

That place where I will honor You
No matter WHAT may come,
Where I can say, with all doubts crushed,
"FATHER, THY WILL BE DONE."

Proverbs 3:5

July 2012

Background of "Higher Ground"

This poem is about a precious woman in our congregation. When we first began attending our church, I would hear many people talking about Debbie, asking me, "You haven't met Debbie yet? You're going to love her!" I hadn't had the opportunity to meet this lady because she had been in the hospital for a long time with a serious illness. Then one Sunday, there she was. I found myself looking into crystal-clear blue eyes, reflecting the light of His love. It only took a short time to realize that she is a pillar of inspiration as she walks out her faith, not because circumstances are perfect but rather *in spite* of circumstances. She *knows* her Knight in shining armor is walking by her side in *every* season.

You Cried With Me

On the darkest of my days,
When *no* light was to be found,
You stepped into the silence,
Providing Peace Profound.

And You Cried with me.

I was a terrified child,
Sobbing in the night.
As darkness tried to smother me,
You Lifted me into Your Light.

And You Cried with me.

When I lay in the dump of insecurity,
The stench of worthlessness all around,
You saw me in that rubble,
Bringing me from being lost to being found.

And You Cried with me.

When trust and love were shattering
Like glass within my heart,
You showed me there was promise,
That there *would* be a brand new start.

And You Cried with me.

When my future was filled with fear,
When I could no longer see the sun,
You showed me double rainbows,
The revelation of things to come.

And You Cried with me.

In spaces filled with emptiness,
As loved ones left this earthly place,
You turned my eyes to Heaven
To see Eternity, where reunion waits.

And You Cried with me.

Ripped relationships torn from the quilt of forever,
Leaving me frozen in my grief,
The warmth of Your Love slowly melting the ice
As it flowed into the river of release,

And You Cried with me.

Wounding words and ongoing offenses,
Could my ruptured heart ever be repaired?
Holding it gently within Your Hands,
Your Touch wiped away *all* my despair.

And You Cried with me.

An earthly father fell far short
Of what a father's love is meant to be,
Yet for *him* I have forgiveness,
Just as *You* have Forgiven *me.*

The image of a father
Is to love and to forgive
As he guides his child onto the path
Where life is truly lived.

As his child's eyes flood with pain,
His heart is also breaking.
Tightly bound within our own concerns,
We sometimes fail to realize the difference this is making.

For it is one thing to be present,
To listen and to care,
But when tears are *intermingled,*
There is a bond beyond compare.

And so, my Jesus,

As my spirit journeys back
To that place it all began,
I feel My Father's Arms around me,
Assuring me of *who* I am.

I am a precious child,
Loved and cherished beyond belief.
From *every* storm and *every* trial
I have *always* found relief.

Because

You, My Father, Have Cried with me.

2 Corinthians 6:18

July 2012

Note on "You Cried With Me"

In prayer one day, I was struck with the realization that, in all my times of tests, trials, and torments, the Lord had not only been there right *beside* me, He had not only *listened* to me, He had been *crying* with me. Our tears had intermingled. I knew in that moment that *each* and *every* tear I had ever shed had fallen into His cupped hands, that *my* pain has been *His* pain. Seeing a glimpse of the depth of His love has left me in awe, and it is the very same love He has for *you*.

Trust

Father, Questions are clattering against each other
Like dominoes in my mind.
As they fall one after another,
There are no answers I can find,

No answers that would point to *You.*
All seems dependent on the world's ways.
How can I afford to believe in the unseen
To plan the course of all my days?

What if? and *How can?* and *Where are You, God?*
Questions shrieking inside my soul,
I look to people, places, and things
To try to make me whole,

To try to fix what looks so unfixable,
To repair what looks so shattered,
To build back a love that once was,
That now seems not to have mattered.

Hopeless in my pain,
Faithless in my walk,
I am sinking in my sorrow,
Seeing despair in all I have sought.

As the spirit lies crushed and broken
Upon the floor of this dark place,
A flickering flame approaches,
Bringing Light into this pitch-black space.

A Voice of Infinite Peace
Breaks through the suffocating deafness,
And as each Word echoes softly,
It leaves the hearer breathless:

"My child,

"Following in My Footsteps
Means to *trust* in where I Lead,
Relying on My Promise
To fulfill your every need,

"*Leaning* on My Staff of Love
To sustain you in your doubts,
Focusing on The Light within
Rather than the darkness that is without.

"When the vice of frantic fear
Grips the hinges of your heart,
You will look to *Me* to find release
Before your heart has fallen apart,

"For The Holy Spirit is Drawing out
The putrid air of disbelief,
Replacing it with *Truth* and *Clarity*,
The *refreshment* of release.

"You must *trust Me* in all seasons;
You must *trust Me* through all trials.
You must *trust Me* with your life,
Or you will drown beneath denials.

"Your heart must *never* slumber;
Your spirit must *forever* seek.
You must keep your ears attuned to hear
To keep from growing weak.

"*Trust in Me* is made of substance
That will *never* burn within the fire.
Trust in Me will never drag you down;
It will *always* lift you higher.

"*Trust* means it is all you have,
Yet It is *all* you will ever need.
Through *trust* you plant a harvest
As you fill the field seed by seed.

"When others see the fruit
That has been produced inside your life,
They will ask how you surmounted
All the *tears,* the *grief,* the *strife.*

"It is then that you can tell them
It was *I* Who satisfied your thirst.
You *listen, seek,* and *trust;*
In your *trust* You have placed Me first.

"When the earth is quaking under you,
When you can barely stand,
Remember I Am The Rock;
I Am The Great I Am.

"Your heart is held within My Hands
No matter *what* may come.
Trust in Me forever,
For it is through your trust that My Will is Done."

2 Samuel 22:31–33

July 2012

Note on "Trust"

Trust: the foundation of every relationship, the bond that holds two hearts together, the ability to believe that no matter *what* circumstances may look like, all things *will* work together for good. He has said it, and we believe Him because of trust. In the times in my life when I have had nothing else to hold onto but my trust in Him, He has never disappointed me. He has been there for me, and He will be there for *you*.

The Promise

Father, How fast can a heart race
Before it collapses inside a chest?
Frantically, I search for an escape,
To know which way is best.

My mind is moving back in time
To the beginning of our days,
When the future looked so bright
As we set out on our way.

A promise of forever
Was made between us two.
To imagine it would be shattered
Is something I could never do.

I thought this promise was protected,
Wrapped in the words *to love, to honor, and to cherish.*
I never envisioned it could become so battered,
To the point that it would perish.

What began as two in unison
Has now been split to only one.
Now storm clouds cover my life
Where once I had the sun.

Yet, In the darkness of this dilemma
I know I am not alone,
For now I have children by my side
Who *need* a loving home.

But our "home" has become a prison
With bars on windows and every door.
There is only *one* thought that I hold secure:
"I can't take this any more!"

Father, I have no answers,
Only questions *quaking* inside my soul.
Where to go and *what to do*
To maybe, someday, feel whole?

I did my best to shut my eyes
To what I didn't want to see.
I walked inside my "blindness"
And lost all sight of me.

My flesh just became frozen
To all of the attacks.
I took each one that came,
Never *daring* to look back.

Because in looking back I would have seen;
A choice to *stand* should have been made.
In my acceptance of what was happening,
There was a very *high* price being paid.

But now the day has come
When there are *no* choices left.
The times of torture are over;
My mind has now been *set.*

I know that what was to be forever
Must now come to an end.
This "relationship" has been ripped to shreds;
There is *nothing* left to mend.

Buried in bitterness and forsaking forgiveness,
The door to these marriage vows will shut.
I have decided beyond a shadow of doubt
That all ties of "together" will be cut.

Yet, In the stillness of this suffering,
A gentle Voice is heard,
His Heart *Pleading* for patience
To let long-lost love be stirred.

"My child,

"Can you remember back
To the moment you first met?
Nothing could keep you apart
As on your path together you were so set.

"To walk together throughout each year,
In the good times as well as the bad,
To uplift, To love through *all* circumstances,
In the happy as well as the sad.

"Yet now, In *this* very moment,
You have nothing left to say.
My ministering angels will go with you
As you continue on your way.

"But should you choose to think again
Of the good that you have shared,
I will shower My Love upon you both
In a way you *cannot* compare.

"Your choice you see as crystal-clear
As you draw a picture of your new life.
Its lines are *very* definite;
Your perspective seems so *precise*.

"But did you draw it through *My* Eyes?
No, My child, It is not so.
For if you had seen what is in *My* Gaze,
Now you would fully *know*

"*That forgiveness is far-reaching.*

"*Despite* the condemnation,
Despite the guilt and shame,
If you look to *Me* for answers,
You *must* lay down all the blame,

"For I will Tell you
That Love lives on, *No matter* what has been done.
I Speak of The Love that comes from My Heart,
The Love that first joined two as one.

"*This* Love is filled with forgiveness,
And as I Hold it out to you,
Recognize Me as The Great I Am;
I Am The Promise Who can make ALL things new."

Revelation 21:5

July 2012

Note on "The Promise"

In "The Promise," the Lord reaches down to place His hand upon a marriage that is about to come to an end. Heartaches that have built up through the years have seemed to smother anything of good that was ever shared between this couple, and this is exactly where the enemy wants their focus to stay, on *every* emotional and physical disappointment that has ever occurred during their time together, as he develops his plan to add one more shattered family to his list.

Yet, inside the broken hearts, the Father of Unconditional Love is gently speaking, offering restoration, hope, and the promise that He *can* make *all* things *new*. He *can* create *beauty* where there only appears to be ashes; He *can* take a broken bond and fortify it with the fire of faith and trust. He can, *if* He is given the opportunity.

Which Way?

My life has been a maze
Of so many mixed-up places.
I tried to find my own way,
But I got lost within the faces.

Easier to be led by the group
Than to think all on my own,
I follow blindly, *anywhere,*
Until my heart has turned to stone.

The innocent child I had once been
Was lost so *long* ago.
I look in the mirror, and staring back
Is somebody I don't know.

Though family and friends *tried* to rescue me,
I could not hear what they said,
For though I walk and talk and breathe,
I am one of the living dead.

Sometimes I catch a glimpse
Of where I have been led:
A deep, dark pit filled with nothingness,
Where my flesh is being fed.

My flesh, But where is the rest of me?
Where is my spirit and my soul?
I feel like I've been torn in pieces
And that I can *never* again be whole.

I feel myself *falling, falling* into endless emptiness,
Where there is *nothing* solid around.
In the pitch-blackness of this bottomless pit,
There is *no* standing ground.

Suddenly, Inside the stench of the deafening stillness,
I hear the devil's shriek of glee,
Screaming, *"Of course you cannot find your soul—*
Did you forget you have given it to me?

"One less sinner for me to think about,
You have already dug your grave.
In your *willingness* to follow the pack,
You have now become *my* slave!

"Your so-called friends that you follow,
They all belong to me!
Haven't you seen they do all in the shadows?
Or have you just been too *blind* to see?

"My craving is *ravenous* for the youth,
To sink my teeth into each one,
For as I destroy their futures,
They will see *no* kingdom come.

"Discouragement, despair, what's the use?
These are all part of *my* song.
Keep playing it over in your mind;
You will be *finished* before too long."

As the slithering snake that is Satan
Ponders with relish his soon-to-be plunder,
He hears in the distance
A sound like rolling thunder.

Just at the moment he is ready
To yank the last bits of faith from this falling youth,
God's Mighty Voice Reverberates
As It rings out with the *Truth:*

"Devil of deception!
The youth belong to *ME.*
Get your claws out of *each* one;
From them you *MUST* now flee!

"Though their flesh has become weakened
For a moment, through your scheme,
I Am filling their spirits with Light;
They will *awaken* from your dark dream.

"Though you sent your demons to destroy
All the good that has been done,
Your lies I Will *crush* to bits;
The Victory is already Won!

"Your fiery darts of deception
Will no longer find their mark
Their eyes have been *re-opened*
To My Hand upon their hearts.

"The future of the youth
Rests within My Hands;
Go back into your pit.
You have *nothing* in this plan.

"They are *Mine,* and they will *know* it
This time, *once and for all.*
They will *stand* steadfast in my purpose,
For they have *clearly* heard My Call."

Now, As this youth looks in the mirror,
He sees another Face.
Next to him is Jesus,
And His Eyes are *Filled* with Grace.

In this moment, the youth *knows*
There is no more time to waste.
He *must* make a decision
Right now, Right here, Right in this very place.

Will he renounce the way of flesh
To walk within The Light?
To stand and dance inside the sunshine
Rather than to creep and crawl inside the night?

And so, To every youth The question is now made:

Will it be *yes,* Or will it be *no?*
There is only *one* way you can go.
The choice belongs to you.
Will your River of Redemption dry up, Or will it flow?

Which way will you go?

Psalm 1:6

July 2012

Note on "Which Way?"

The poem "Which Way?" expresses the urgency for our youth to take a stand, once and for all, for Jesus. It is an obvious fact that Satan's goal is to destroy them, and it is easy to see why. When we see youth taking a stand for Christ, something stirs within our spirit. It speaks of hope, it speaks of promise, it speaks of a future built upon The Rock of Ages, a place where the plan of the enemy is frozen and the kingdom of our Father reigns. Let Your kingdom come, Lord!

The Invitation

"Come follow Me," You Whispered,
As these poems had their start.
I heard You within my spirit;
I *followed* You with my heart.

The words flowed like a fountain
From Your Throne in Heaven's Realm.
There is no other explanation,
For from *me* they surely did not come.

I *will* follow You, My Jesus,
In all things, big and small.
I *will* follow You forever,
For I have heard Your Call.

And so, dear reader, As you finish these last pages,
As you come to the last lines of this prose,
My prayer is that you have been blessed
And Touched by The Holy Spirit's Glow.

Though this book does have a closing,
These poems will never have an end,
For they were meant to touch the spirit
And into Eternity extend.

They were meant for *you*, for *me*,
To draw ever closer to His Love,
To know He Lives *within* us,
Not just some place up above.

To give us *hope* in sorrow,
To give us *strength* to wait,
To set our eyes on Heaven
As we look upon its Gate,

To know our sight must be on Him
In *all* we say and do,
To know He Is our Father
And He will *always* See us through,

Through *all* the trials that we may face,
Through *all* our deepest fears,
Through *every* moment of day and night
As they melt into the years.

Maybe you haven't heard Him near,
As the noise of this world drowned out His knock.
Maybe you haven't been able to see His Face
Through the deep darkness this world has brought.

But He is *Closer* than the air you breathe;
He is brighter than the sun.
His Love for *you* is *endless;*
You are His *precious* one.

He is Inviting you with *all* His Heart
To *please* draw near to Him,
No matter what you've done,
No matter where you've been.

As you hear His gentle Calling
At the doorway of your heart,
Say this simple prayer;
Your new life will have its start:

Jesus, I repent of my sins.

Come into my life;
I make *You* my Lord and Savior.
From this moment on, I belong to *You.*
From *Your* path I will no longer waiver.

Psalm 34:8

July 2012

CPSIA information can be obtained at www.ICGtesting.com
Printed in the USA
BVOW011247100113

310220BV00002B/5/P